The Survivor's Quest

The Survivor's Quest

Recovery After

Encountering Evil

by HealingJourney

ISBN: 1500418854
ISBN-13: 978-1500418854

Cover design by damonza.com

For all who have taught me about true love,
in its many forms

"Wherever you go, go with all your heart."

~Confucius

CONTENTS

PHASE THREE: MORE LIGHT THAN DARK

Introduction

Encountering Evil

If you are reading this book, then I imagine you have been touched by evil, in the form of psychopathic abuse. It is an experience that has the potential to destroy one's soul. But...it does not have to! I am a survivor of an encounter with psychopathic evil. The "relationship"—specifically, the end of it—devastated me and threw me into a period of intense despair. For a long time, I believed I would *always* be hurting. And I did hurt, for what seemed like an eternity. Thankfully, I received amazing support from others who have "open eyes," from my therapist, and from the special people in my life who offered me real love before, during, and after the trauma. With their help,

I was able to find my way out of the pain. I learned how to believe in myself at a deeper level and trust in the truth of what happened to me. Now, my life is filled with many moments of joy, peace, and gratitude, more than I ever thought were possible!

You may be overwhelmed by pain at this particular moment, and my heart goes out to you. I remember how hopeless I felt. I assure you that you, too, can find your way out of the pain, and you, too, can discover much light and love on the other side of the darkness. If you are still involved with an abuser (a psychopath, sociopath, narcissist, or other disordered person), perhaps this book will give you the tools you need to break free. If you have escaped, or if you have been discarded (like I was), I hope that you will find comfort in what I have written. No matter where you are on your healing journey, you have come to the right place.

As is the case with all survivors, the details of what happened during my time with the psychopath could fill an entire book. My intention is not to write a memoir, but to instead provide tips on how to recover during the aftermath of the encounter. However, I also found that reading the stories of others helped me tremendously with my own healing. So, because it may be helpful, I am including a short version of my story below. If you read it, I urge you not to be concerned about the differences that may exist between our stories. Focus on the eerie similarities, even if there are only a few, because that is where important truths lie.

My (Brief) Story

I met the psychopath via an online dating website. He sent me a nice message, we talked on the phone the next day, and then the texting began. He was smooth and did not overdo it. He knew just how to dose the flattery so that I felt comfortable with him. He also stretched out the texts and the phone conversations for two weeks until finally scheduling a time to meet with me in person. Our relationship developed quickly from that point, and I remember feeling so happy! In general, especially in the beginning, he spent regular time with me, usually about three to four days per week.

As the months went on, that time together lessened, and he was very creative in terms of varying the excuses he gave for not being able to visit me. I offered to come to his place, but he told me he did not mind making the trip to see me. And although I met his friends a few times, most of the time we socialized with my friends, all of whom liked him. He charmed everyone. About four months into our encounter, I started to ask him why I had not met his parents. He put me off for a few more months, but I finally met them. It was the first and last time that would happen. Clearly, he was keeping a wall up.

Our time together continued, and although he was always pleasant to my face, and although he told me daily that he loved me, I felt worried about the future of our relationship. It seemed as if he did not want to make a commitment. But, he assured me he loved me, and I cared about him deeply. I also felt that he was such a great match for me, so I pushed my worries aside. After about a year of dating, we made plans for him to move in with me. But when the time came, he told me he needed to delay the move in date. He seemed to have a good excuse, although I told him I was upset that he had not consulted me first.

Several weeks later, he assured me he would move in the following weekend, and then all of a sudden, he said he had gone to the doctor, had been diagnosed with anxiety, and needed time by himself (e.g., the entire weekend). I had a horrible feeling in the pit of my stomach, but I accepted his excuse at the time because he had always mirrored my introversion. Looking back now, it is obvious that he was lying to me and that his weekend away was a weekend spent with another woman. However, he had told me from the beginning that his ex-girlfriend had cheated on him, so it simply did not occur to me that, in reality, he was a completely different person from the one he portrayed himself to be.

After that weekend, his anxiety morphed into depression. For two more months, he broke promise after promise, using the "depression" as a cover. He continued to be "nice" to me to my face, however, even though I was telling him that I felt worried and angry about the ways in which he was pulling away from me.

Finally, he told me over the phone that he could not see me anymore and needed time to get better, and then we could try again. I remember how very emotionless he sounded in that last conversation. He said he wanted to text with me—of course—but I refused and decided to take some space from him (minus a brief text apology I sent him two days later, regarding how "mean" I was to him during our breakup conversation). However, I was concerned about him because of the "depression" and because of the abrupt end to our supposed relationship. So a week later, I went on Facebook to look for the profile of one of the psychopath's friends. My intention was to check on him by contacting one of his friends. I did not have any phone numbers for anyone connected with him, and I did not want to text him, so Facebook was my best option.

In the process of looking up the friend, I accidentally discovered the psychopath's Facebook profile, which I did not even know existed, since he had told me from the beginning that he had closed it down. On the profile, I noticed that he was "in a relationship" with someone, and it certainly was not me. I clicked on the name, and that is when I saw the other woman's profile picture, which was a picture of her with the psychopath. The truth—he was a liar and cheater—came crashing down on me, and I was stunned. I also discovered that their relationship had started almost three months before that; yet during that time he had assured me that I was "the love of his life." And I remember that was the day that the word "evil" came to my mind, very suddenly, which had never happened to me before, in any other situation. It was the best word to describe his behavior and the devastating betrayal.

I confronted him via text that day with what I had discovered, because he did not answer my phone call. He did text me back, and it was the very last time I interacted with him. Then, the other woman found my phone number and reached out to me briefly a couple days later. I learned from her that he had been married twice, which I did not know, and he had cheated on me with other women, as well. Although speaking with her was very painful and not something I recommend, especially because she decided to stay with him, she sent me something via text that has helped me immensely in my attempts to make sense out of what happened. She wrote, "He says he knows he was a monster to an innocent person." I did not appreciate it at the time, but it was the best psychopathic tell I could have ever received.

Book Organization

I settled on an imperfect structure for this book in the form of the "phases" of a survivor's quest. They outline a possible search for truth and path out of the darkness. The three phases are each broken down into three to four topics that, in general, characterize each phase. Please note that I am basing much of the content on what I learned during my own recovery, and it is likely that not everyone will be able to relate to everything I share. I have tried to present the content in such a way so that it applies to as many survivors as possible, but each reader is encouraged to take away that which resonates and leave the rest. In addition, considerable overlap exists between the elements describing each phase and between the phases themselves. As experts on grief have explained time and again, the healing process is not linear. It is not neat and tidy. We take one step forward, two steps back, three steps forward, one step back, and so on. There is also no specific timeline for how long the phases should last. They should be viewed as fluid and flexible.

Sharing My Journey

My only credentials for writing this book come from my own experiences. I have read extensively about the topic of psychopathy, but I am not an expert on it. And despite a strong interest in psychology and a commitment to regular, quiet introspection, I am also not a therapist. I am a teacher of young children.

But, I am certainly a survivor, and I have transformed my life in spite of what happened with the psychopath, not because of it. I hope that by sharing what I have learned across the course of my recovery journey, I can help others find ways to develop self-love and a new, positive belief in humanity. Although my brush with evil was in the context of a romantic relationship, psychopathic abuse has important similarities across individual situations. I am hopeful that this book will be accessible for everyone who has been targeted, whether it was by a lover, a colleague, a friend, or a family member.

I decided to use a pseudonym, due to the subject matter and in order to protect my safety and the safety of others. I am writing under the username I chose for an internet forum, PsychopathFree. When I registered for the forum, I was so anxious to share my story and connect with others who understood what I was going through that I came up with the name in a hurry, and at first, I regretted my choice. But then, after I wrote my very first post, I was immediately welcomed by one of the members, Peace (also known as Jackson), who told me that he loved the name. That gesture of kindness had an incredibly positive effect on me—more than words can express. It marked a turning point in my recovery, and "HealingJourney" has been an important part of who I am ever since that moment.

Readers, may you find validation and hope as you travel on this quest with me.

~HealingJourney

PHASE ONE:
OPEN EYES

"The real meaning of enlighten-
ment is to gaze with undimmed
eyes on all darkness."

~Nikos Kazantzakis

1
Illusion

Letting Go of the Dream

Psychopathic predators specialize in creating an extremely intoxicating illusion. They do it by tuning in to their targets' hopes and dreams, personalities, strengths, weaknesses, insecurities, and deepest desires. Somehow, they seem to know their targets better than the targets know themselves. Once they have assessed their new supply, they then turn themselves into the (almost) perfect mirror images of their victims and reflect back just what the victims are looking for in terms of a "soul mate."

Psychopaths shower their targets with flattery; they put them on pedestals and make them feel as if

they are on top of the world. In the context of romantic relationships, powerful chemicals that facilitate
attachment are released in victims' brains during sex,
which makes it even easier for psychopaths to get
what they want. But the idealization process need not
involve sex; it can happen in all sorts of relationships.
And it need not involve daily gifts or constant text
messages. Psychopaths seem to know how to provide
just enough attention and adoration in order to
"hook" their targets and create terrifyingly strong
bonds. The bonds are terrifying because they are
based on lies.

I remember the beginning of my time with the
psychopath very well. I had always felt that most
people did not understand me, and when I met him, I
was amazed that he "got" me so quickly! We had all of
the right things in common; he was everything I was
looking for, and then some! It almost felt too good to
be true. And in fact, it *always was* too good to be
true. As in every psychopathic encounter, the "connection" we had—the connection he specifically told
me we had, the connection he emphasized as important and special—was an illusion. His idealization
of me was not real, it had never been real, and so it
could not last. Cracks began to appear in his unique

understanding of me, until it finally all came crashing down. I thought I had met my "dream man;" yet in reality I had loved my own reflection, a distorted one created by the psychopath.

But, not all of it was a lie. I was real, and my feelings were real. Somehow, in the midst of the intense pain I felt after the discard, I held on to the little bit of light that was left in my soul, the light that told me I was worthy of real love, and this was **not** it! When I was able to focus on that truth, I was able to let go of the fantasy that I had found the "love of my life." And incredibly, letting go of the illusion brought me closer to my own heart.

You may find it extremely difficult to believe that the admiration and "love" the psychopath offered you was never real. That truth is what makes it so difficult to even begin to move forward from an encounter with a toxic person. If you are still involved with a psychopath, or if you are tempted to return to an abuser, the power of the dream is one reason why it is so hard to break free. And it is one reason why you may have returned to that person over and over again, especially if you were reassured by the psychopath that any mistreatment was an aberration.

Sadly and unfortunately, the image you have in your mind of the person you loved is a cruel lie—that person never existed. He or she was only a mask that the psychopath generated in order to manipulate you. So, as crushingly hard as it is and as much as it hurts, the only way to find freedom, the only way to start the healing process, is to stop believing in that person. Do your very best to let go of the dream. Because when you let go, that is when you will start to find the real you.

Cognitive Dissonance

As you begin to let go of the dream, you will be faced with the next big recovery hurdle: cognitive dissonance. For me, cognitive dissonance was the most frustrating and disorienting challenge that I endured during my journey. It is difficult to define, but in the context of breaking free from an abusive relationship, cognitive dissonance is the battle that your brain wages in trying to reconcile two completely different visions of who the psychopath really is. On one hand, you have the idealized image of your soul mate, the illusion the psychopath created in order to mirror and exploit you. And on the other hand, you have an opposite and evil image, a picture that has begun to appear through the cracks in the psychopath's mask. The effects of this inner war inside your head are intense feelings of confusion and pain. You feel as if you are literally in some sort of fog, and this is one reason why you may feel like you are going crazy.

Cognitive dissonance is also exacerbated by the fact that, before experiencing evil, most people automatically believe that there *must* be some sort of good in absolutely everyone. The frightening truth is that some people are permanently worthless and rotten to the core, and they are often very, very good at hiding it.

Although I *knew* something was terribly wrong with the psychopath's behavior, and although the word "evil" had found its way into my consciousness, I repeatedly questioned my memories of what happened during and after the encounter. At times, I was convinced that I was imagining all of it. I was convinced that I must be in the middle of a horrible dream, because only in a nightmare would someone be so despicable. But as time went on, I realized that the nightmare was my daily life. I realized I had no hope of escape, and I began to accept that the evil I felt from the psychopath was real.

My struggle with cognitive dissonance consisted of many instances like the one described above, during which I fought with myself and doubted my own perceptions. Because of the negative effects of the psychopath's lies on my brain, that inner war lasted a long time. At first, I faced the difficult task of accepting that the psychopath never loved me. Then, as that reality began to sink in, I wondered if the lying and cheating were normal human behaviors. I wondered if, perhaps, my expectations that honesty and monogamy should be givens in a relationship were completely unrealistic. It took me months to finally believe, without a doubt, that those expectations *were* normal.

On top of that, the psychopath was always "nice" to me to my face, and he never tried to contact me after the discard. These two facts from my story differed significantly from most other survivor stories, so I was continuously tormented by the "Is he a psychopath?" question. But I kept reading story after story; I had a compulsion to do it, so I did. I wanted desperately to clear my head! And in the end, my reading of others' stories, along with my realization that **it was the unbelievable similarities that truly mattered**, ultimately served as the keys to conquering the cognitive dissonance.

Your experience with cognitive dissonance may be different from mine, and as you read the stories of others (please see the Appendix for recommended resources that can help you do that), you will notice variations between their stories and yours. This happens because psychopaths themselves are different from each other (in some ways), and survivors are certainly very different from each other. The story variations are endless and can include issues such as the length of the relationship, the precise nature of the abuse, and the presence or absence of stalking and "hoovering" attempts. These differences may cause you to wonder if you are wrong to be suspicious of the psychopath. You may think, "That did not happen to me, so maybe he or she really does love me! Maybe he or she really is a good person going through a bad time." It can be very hard to ignore those differences and focus on the strange and frightening similarities instead. You may be like me and want someone to tell you, in absolute terms, whether or not the person who abused you is a psychopath.

Unfortunately, no one can give you a definite answer to the "Is he or she a psychopath?" question. However, if you can relate to what I am writing, then I hope that you will trust in that and allow it to guide you. I also offer more information in the next chapter, regarding how psychopaths operate, that may help you answer that question. One thing is certain: it is a difficult process to clear the fog from your mind. And ultimately, the most important step toward doing that is to get away from the abuser.

No Contact

Most survivors have a very hard time implementing the No Contact rule, so if you are struggling with it, please know that you *are* normal, and you are also not alone! Despite the difficulties, it is essential that you cut off contact with the psychopath, as much as possible and as soon as possible. I realize some of you may have children with the psychopath, or you may be in a situation that forces you to be in contact, somehow, with the person who abused you. Please refer to the link to the "Gray Rock" article in the Appendix for tips on how to handle those particular situations. But if you are in the position to get away completely, then I urge you to do it! It is very hard, absolutely, but it **can** be accomplished. I offer suggestions below for how you can break free and stay free.

I am about to write some difficult truths that may

be very painful for you to read. I want to reassure you that, despite those hard truths, there **is** light on the other side of the darkness, so stay with me! I have already revealed one effective and powerful way in which to find the strength to cut the psychopath out of your life and stick to it: let go of the illusion that you have found the perfect partner for you. This can be especially hard if you have a sexual relationship with an abusive person. As mentioned above, the chemicals released in the brain during sex enhance feelings of attachment. However, only targets feel an emotional attachment. Psychopaths do not. That is why it is so important to stop having sex with the abuser; it will allow your mind to clear.

Another practical suggestion that can help you start and then maintain No Contact is to write down everything that the psychopath did to hurt you. Write down anything and everything he or she did that upset and bothered you, even if it is something that seems insignificant. Read and reread your list. I did this, and it was one of the best healing strategies I used. It also helped me work through the cognitive dissonance.

When you begin to believe that you were never loved, and you start to see how much you were used and violated, you will feel disgust, and you will feel rage. In some ways, the disgust and rage make you feel as if you never want to see the psychopath again. And yet, in other ways, they tempt you to seek out revenge against the abuser. In my case, I wanted to send nasty letters to the psychopath. I even wanted to confront him in person and hurt him physically! And, after I went on the truth-finding mission that I will describe in the next chapter, I wanted to contact the other woman and tell her what I had discovered about him. It was very, very hard to stop myself, but I did. And the **only reason** I found the strength to do that was because I really saw the evil in him—I felt it deeply, just as I had the moment I found the picture of him with the other woman—and it scared me.

As I tuned in to those feelings, I knew that, if I interfered with his life and his relationship with the other woman, he was capable of hurting me in ways I did not even want to imagine. The fear kept me safe, because I listened to it. I will elaborate on how to process emotions and tune in to intuition later, but for now I hope that you will listen carefully to any discomfort and fear you may feel.

About a month or so into my own No Contact time, I had a reassuring breakthrough. I realized that

I had taken control back from the psychopath by shutting him out of my life. He will never again know what I am doing, thinking, or feeling, and although that will not hurt him, it also prevents him from playing more games with me. This realization did not magically alleviate my pain, but it did help me stay away from him. I hope that you, too, will begin to view No Contact as a wonderful way in which to take back your life. It truly is your key to freedom.

I realize that the implementation of these strategies may not prevent you from experiencing the temptation to reach out to the psychopath, probably because you feel as if you are being torn apart by excruciating pain. You may believe that contacting him or her will relieve the pain, and for a moment, it may. In the end, however, the pain will return and be even more severe. Contact opens the door for the psychopath to play with your mind and crush your heart further, and it makes the cognitive dissonance worse. Therefore, the more you can see and accept the truth that the psychopath never cared for you and was intentionally trying to hurt you, the easier it will be to stay away. And by sticking with No Contact, you will begin to heal.

And yet, even after you cut off all communication

with the abuser, and even after you make progress in your healing, it is highly likely that you will be tempted to find out what is happening in the psychopath's life, and you may not be able to stop yourself. Social media makes this especially easy. I confess that I looked up the psychopath several times on Facebook, and each time I viewed his profile, it set me back slightly in my recovery. Each time, it felt like someone was jabbing a small knife into my heart. However, I forgave myself for these mistakes. And I blocked him (and the other woman) when I was ready. So do your best to stay away from the psychopath who hurt you, as much as you can. If you have a setback, it really is okay. Just keep moving forward.

Letting go of the illusion, understanding the effects of cognitive dissonance, and eliminating contact with the psychopath all mark the beginning of your recovery. Unfortunately, you will still have what seems to be a long healing road ahead of you, and most likely, you will be plagued by one question in particular: "WHY?"

2
WHY?

A Truth-Finding Mission

When I abruptly discovered the psychopath's betrayal, I immediately found myself tormented by so many "why" questions, specifically about why the psychopath did what he did. **WHY** did he lie so much? **WHY** did he work so hard to convince me that he loved me, only to discard me so callously? **WHY** did he spend so much time with me, if he never, ever cared for me? **WHY** did he keep things going with me as he pursued other "relationships"? **WHY** did he suddenly turn into a completely different person?

Perhaps even more frustrating than the questions themselves were the responses I received from others as I attempted to find answers. I was told that the questions could not be answered. I was told that I should definitely not go on what I call my "truth-finding mission." I was told that it was not a good idea (in other words, it was unhealthy) to think about the psychopath and about psychopathy in general. I was told, time and again and in one way or another, "Focus on you."

Somehow, I was able to ignore such unhelpful advice. I realized that I was deeply compelled to find answers to the questions and to find out as much of the truth about the psychopath as I could. And I realized that these compulsions were not only okay, they were *essential* to my recovery. I **was** focusing on me, despite what others assumed.

When I began my investigation of the specific abuser who hurt me, everyone in my life—really, *everyone*—discouraged me from learning anything new about him. But I went ahead with my search. I had an overwhelming need to uncover as many lies as possible. I am thankful that I conducted it without making contact with the psychopath or anyone connected with him; the No Contact rule kept me safe. And when I exhausted every anonymous avenue available to me, I stopped. I uncovered only a portion of the truth, but the little bit I discovered helped me see him for the monster that he admitted he is.

My general research about psychopathy was separate from my specific truth-finding mission regarding the psychopath, and my "obsession" with the larger topic of psychopathy continued for a long time. In fact, the strong desire I had to find out *what* he is, exactly, was important and necessary. I wanted a specific label for him, and I wanted a specific definition with specific traits. I found that reading just one book about psychopathy was not enough. I needed to read information from a variety of sources in order to wrap my brain around such foreign and disturbing concepts.

When I mentioned to others what I was learning about personality disorders, I heard the warnings to let it go and move on. I noticed the concerned and slightly patronizing looks. But I continued with my studies, despite the discomfort of being so misunderstood. In the end, I realized that this ongoing research was an incredibly powerful way to find myself again.

You can find yourself again too, and one way to do that is to give yourself permission to research this topic and to investigate the psychopath who targeted you, as safely as you can. Listen to what your heart is telling you. If you feel compelled to read, write, and think about psychopathy, then listen to that and follow it. I assure you, it is not possible to "think too much." I will discuss obsessive thoughts and trauma in a later chapter, and I will offer suggestions for finding peace, but my point here is that you should give yourself permission to "obsess" about this, despite what others may tell you.

Although it is impossible to emotionally understand how psychopaths think—and no normal person would want to—it **is** possible to understand them at an intellectual level. By learning how psychopaths operate, you will develop new wisdom. Understanding the psychopathic mind will also give you new power. It will help you realize that the abuse was never your fault! And when you begin to see that and start to believe it, then you will find that you have already made remarkable progress in your recovery.

Below, I provide an overview of what experts have discovered about psychopathic traits and how psychopaths think and operate.

Understanding Psychopaths

Psychopathy lies on a spectrum

Psychopaths are not easily identified. In fact, it can be exceptionally difficult to determine if someone is a psychopath. Even professionals are easily fooled, and many counselors have a poor understanding of personality disorders in general. In addition, some people exhibit more psychopathic traits than others, which is why psychopathy lies on a spectrum. Some psychopathic people are very obviously egotistical, for example; others are much more covert in their narcissism. That is just one example of the differences. Perhaps this is why several terms have been used to describe people who exhibit abnormal personality traits, including psychopath, sociopath, and narcissist. To further add to the confusion, psychologists, therapists, and researchers do not agree on which terms should be used or how they should be defined. Despite this controversy, the fact remains that a person who exhibits any number of psychopathic traits is toxic and should be avoided.

Psychopaths lack a conscience

Psychopaths know the intellectual difference between right and wrong. They understand society's expectations. They understand what moral behavior is supposed to look like. They even understand that actions have consequences. The problem is that they *do not care*. They do not feel remorse or guilt. They have no inner compass to guide them, and so they do exactly what they want at any given moment. This lack of conscience means that it does not matter to them if they trample on the rights, feelings, or safety of others. It means that they have no limits and are therefore capable of anything; it is a recipe for endless cruelty and depravity.

Psychopaths feel a limited range of human emotions

Psychopaths are plagued by emotional abnormalities, making them empty shells. They experience "shallow" feelings, which means that virtually all of their emotions are fleeting, if they have them at all. They seem to feel rage and envy in full force, which fuels aggressive behavior in many of them. However, any rages they display are surprisingly short-lived.

Because of this defect, psychopaths are unable to truly connect with other people. They are unable to have true empathy for others, they are incapable of compassion, and they <u>do not suffer</u>, because they cannot relate to emotional pain. They live a life devoid of true pleasure, unable to enjoy a sunset or the company of an animal or another person. They only get temporary, meaningless thrills out of things like sex or food or deceiving and manipulating others.

Most ominously, this emotional deficiency means that they are unable to ***love***. It also means that they must spend their entire lives watching others and learning to imitate behaviors that they are unable to engage in naturally; in this way, they become demented chameleons.

Their emptiness also makes them chronically bored. The boredom is almost painful for them, and they will do anything to alleviate it. This contributes to their tendency to act impulsively and recklessly; for instance, it is very common for psychopaths to become addicted to alcohol, sex, and drugs. And ultimately, they will do anything and everything to get rid of their boredom because, having no conscience and no empathy, they do not care who gets hurt in the process.

Psychopaths view everything in life— including relationships—as games to be won

Psychopaths have an insatiable need to win and obtain power and control over their targets. The desire to win is so strong that sometimes they will actually take themselves down in the process of becoming the "winners."

Because they are unable to build real relationships, psychopaths view their interactions with others as games. Other people are simply pawns to be played. And because they have no conscience, they make up their own unethical, ever-changing rules for those "games." They use tactics like mirroring, deception, projection, gaslighting, pity plays, the silent treatment, smear campaigns, and other forms of emotional and physical abuse to idealize, manipulate, confuse, and intimidate others, all in the name of "winning."

Psychopaths live to exploit others

The ultimate purpose of every psychopath's life is

to do whatever it takes to get what he or she wants at that moment. Since psychopaths do not understand love, they view other people as objects to be obtained, used, and then discarded. And so in all their interactions with others, they follow a particular pattern— idealize, devalue, and discard—over and over and over again. They are constantly scoping out potential targets and assessing them as sources of supply. Their desires change unexpectedly and abruptly; at any given moment, they might want money, or a place to live, or sex, or a cloak of normalcy, or a short-term thrill.

They often throw people away suddenly and brutally, ignore them for days, months, or even years, and then contact them again as if no time has passed and all is well. They find it entertaining to lure targets back into their games, if it serves their purposes. Nothing stops them from pursuing whatever they want in any way they can.

Psychopaths provide "tells" about who they really are

Psychopathic tells are yet another manipulation tactic psychopaths use to exploit others. They specialize in playing mind games with others, and tells are an effective way in which to confuse their targets. The tells come in three forms: projections on to others, truthful remarks, and statements that are the exact opposite of the truth.

Projection

When psychopaths project, they are giving their targets camouflaged clues. They talk about how other people cheat or lie or hurt others, as if they abhor such behavior, when in fact they are describing themselves. And during the devalue phase of their "relationships," they often project this negativity on to their targets, in an effort to make their victims doubt themselves. It also has the effect of making targets feel as if they are going crazy.

The Truth

Psychopaths tell their targets exactly who they are, but they do it in such a way that it is impossible for victims to understand the consequences of the horrible statements. Targets might hear comments like, "You shouldn't be with me" or "I've never had a good relationship" or "I wanted to hurt someone."

Psychopaths turn these declarations into pity plays and feel secretly justified in exploiting victims when they do not realize the statements are real.

The Opposite of the Truth

Psychopaths convince their targets that they will never lie or cheat and that they love them so much. They also promise that they will never do anything to hurt their victims. They regularly mislead targets by making claims that are precisely the opposite of the truth.

Psychopaths believe they are superior beings

Psychopaths see nothing wrong with using people and then throwing them away. They feel completely justified in lying, cheating, stealing, and manipulating others. In fact, not only do they see nothing wrong with their behavior, they actually believe that they are incredibly superior to other people! Every time they are able to con their targets, they view that as evidence of the targets' weakness.

And, they do not suffer from low self-esteem or insecurities (although they often pretend to "feel" that way in order to manipulate others). On the contrary, they are egotistical and arrogant. And this makes it impossible for them to benefit from therapy, and it makes it impossible for them to change. Why should they change, when they believe they are already better than everyone else? **This**, I believe, is one important reason why there is *no cure* for psychopathy.

Pathological Lying

All psychopaths use one particular manipulation tactic that deserves an entire section of its own to describe the destruction it causes. That tactic is pathological lying, and it is central to the psychopathic personality. This particular topic is very important to me because, in the beginning of my own recovery, I held on to the one solid piece of truth that I knew about the psychopath: he was a LIAR. I held on tightly to that fact and started to research "pathological lying" on the internet. Unfortunately, I came up with nothing helpful. It was only when I painstakingly found my way to psychopathy that I uncovered accurate answers to my many questions! I eventually realized that pathological lying and psychopathy are inextricably linked.

The above truth is obscured by a popular, and dangerous, assumption that exists within our society; it is even supported by research. That assumption is: **everyone** lies. Since everyone does it, since lying is apparently so universal and typical, it follows that it must not be that bad. Right? Wrong. Yes, almost all of us have told white lies to spare others' feelings or with the intention of protecting others. And normal people lie to hide the shame they feel about wrongdoings or because they fear the consequences of their mistakes. But, there are other people who lie habitually, with the intent to deceive and manipulate others for their own personal gain, and they do not feel bad about doing it. In fact, they revel in it. These people are pathological liars, and they are psychopaths.

After much research, I have concluded that all pathological and compulsive liars have personality disorders, and those disorders can be placed on a psychopathic spectrum. Pathological lying is the opposite of normal. I will repeat that: pathological lying is **the opposite of normal**! It is irrelevant that researchers have discovered evidence that everyone lies in one way or another. Not only are most lies damaging, psychopathic lies are beyond the scope of what most people can even imagine when they think about lying. When someone lies habitually, that behavior pattern is *always* connected to other extremely disturbing traits and behaviors. As Martha Stout wrote in *The Sociopath Next Door*, "Deceit is the linchpin of conscienceless behavior."

Thus, lying is like breathing for psychopaths, and they use it as a manipulation tool in the following ways:

Psychopaths lie in order to dominate others

Because relationships are games to them, and because they view other people as objects and feel completely justified in exploiting them, psychopaths know that deception creates an uneven playing field. Lying is integral to impression management and mirroring; the lies enable psychopaths to present false images of themselves to potential targets. Those targets lose the ability to make safe and appropriate decisions. They enter into the relationships, unaware of the danger in store for them.

Then, once the targets are hooked, psychopaths continue to use lies, along with a sprinkling of truth, in a multitude of ways, to ensure that their targets keep "playing." They lie to cover up cheating, alcoholism, drug use, and sometimes various illegal activities. They lie through evasion and by withholding information. They lie as a form of gaslighting, in order to increase their control over their targets by making them constantly question themselves. They often repeatedly tell **the ultimate lie**, that they "love" their targets. And, they lie *just for the fun of it*.

Psychopaths actually feel a form of pleasure when they lie

Unlike lies told out of fear or to hide shame, psychopathic lies are often told because they bring a shallow form of pleasure to the liar. This is called "Duper's Delight." This explains why psychopaths sometimes lie when it is completely unnecessary or when the truth would be more advantageous. Psychopaths also include a variety of details in their lies, not only because it makes their lies sound more credible, but also because they enjoy constructing a false reality and making others believe it. It feeds their need for power and provides them with sick entertainment.

Psychopaths lie effortlessly and are very convincing

Psychopaths experience pleasure from lying because they lack the normal range of human emotions. They are empty and bored, they lack empathy for others, and they do not feel shame or remorse. This emptiness also enables them to lie with minimal effort. They can look other people straight in the eye and lie quickly and guiltlessly, without flinching, even when confronted with probing questions and evidence of previous deception. It is also easy for them to deny the lies, make up excuses, and project their own behavior on to others, which is, of course, a lie in itself. Although some psychopaths do not bother with apologies, others say they are sorry on a regular basis, and because they say this without feeling any shame, they can come across as sincere.

Psychopaths lie to make others feel sorry for them

All psychopaths know exactly how to elicit sympathy from their targets. They are exploiters, and so they take advantage of the natural desire most people have to help and nurture their fellow human beings. They use deception (and sometimes a smidgeon of truth) to create a plethora of fabricated ailments and problems. Common pity plays include fake illnesses and injuries, along with "crazy" exes, car accidents, and theft, to name just a few.

Psychopaths generate as many pretend sob stories as needed in order to draw others into their hidden games, again and again and again. The ability they have to lie pathologically, easily, and confidently makes it possible for them to convince others that such an implausible number of tragedies is plausible, which unfortunately opens the door to a variety of manipulation and exploitation opportunities.

The process of learning about psychopathy can be very overwhelming. I hope that the above summary helps to clarify some concepts that may be confusing. However, I want to reiterate that I am not an expert, and the overview I have given may not provide the details that you need. I based the content of this chapter on what I learned from the books and websites included in the Appendix, so please consider reading them, as well. It is an unfortunate reality that wrapping our minds around the topic of evil is difficult, time-consuming, and very painful.

3
Pain

Facing Pain

The aftermath of my encounter with the psycho-path produced some of the most intense emotional pain I have ever experienced. I felt permanently dam-aged, broken, and worthless. The worst part was that the horrible pain seemed to be everlasting. For at least two months after the discard, I cried every single day. I also developed insomnia, and I had to push myself to eat a reasonable amount of food. My appe-tite changed so drastically that it caused me to lose ten pounds in a month! It was a struggle to make it through every single day, and all I wanted to do was curl up in a ball and never face the world again. But somehow, I forced myself to go to work on a daily basis. As unhappy as I was with my job at the time, it provided a comforting structure to my life, particularly in those early, difficult days of my recovery. Unfortunately, the teaching was only a temporary distraction; staying busy was a short-term fix. The pain was ultimately still with me.

The attempt I made to retreat into my work in order to find relief was a normal response to pain. All normal human beings try to avoid it. The evidence for this is that we have built-in self-defense mechanisms. Those self-defense mechanisms make a lot of sense; after all, no one wants to suffer. No one wants to hurt. That is why we are all so familiar with the term "denial," and that is why so many people believe that "staying busy" is an excellent strategy for healing. However, the more you try to avoid pain, the more it will find ways to sabotage you, which is why facing it is so vital to recovery.

Paradoxically, when you allow yourself to experience past and current pain, you eventually find long-lasting relief from it. There are no magical fixes, but often the act of courageously opening yourself up to suffering brings comfort more quickly than you might expect. And, even though it is impossible to believe when you are in the middle of the nightmare, on the other side of your deepest suffering is the opportunity to experience the greatest joy!

Although I am emphasizing the importance of facing pain, I am **not** claiming that avoidance behaviors are always bad. Sometimes your body automatically switches on a self-defense mechanism as a default, because if it did not, you would shut down completely and be unable to function due to shock. Therefore, the short-term implementation of avoidance strategies, such as denial and distractions, are sometimes absolutely necessary. When they are used appropriately, they allow you to build up enough strength so that you can process the pain effectively. For example, I have been in a state of denial at various points in my life, and every single instance prepared me for what was to come. However, problems begin to occur when coping strategies meant only for short-term use become long-term solutions.

The process of motivating yourself to face pain begins with how you perceive and process your emotions.

A Range of Emotions

Unlike psychopaths, most human beings experience a range of emotions—joy, sorrow, fear, anger, and so on. We not only experience these feelings, including many more than the four I have listed, but we also feel them **deeply**.

Psychopaths believe that our emotions make us weak, but the opposite is true. Our emotions enable us to build loving relationships with others. They enable us to establish *real* connections. They give us the ability to demonstrate compassion, to build caring communities, to cooperate and collaborate with each other, to appreciate the wonders of nature, and to help others altruistically, without expecting anything in return. I believe that our emotions are **the essence of our humanity**. Although toxic people seem to be able to read their targets so well, they cannot actually understand us at all, because they cannot understand love. And life is nothing without love, because love makes everything that is worthwhile possible. *Only those who experience the full range of emotions are able to love*, which is why our feelings and the ways in which we process them are so important.

I was extremely fortunate to grow up with a

mother who taught me from a very early age that all emotions are okay, even difficult feelings, such as anger and sadness. She was and still is a phenomenal listener, and I remember she would spend a lot of her free time with me, allowing me to talk on and on about anything and everything. She always made me feel understood, and she did it by tuning in to my feelings, whatever they happened to be, and by paraphrasing what I said to confirm that she heard me.

Of course, every person in my family was far from perfect in terms of handling emotions, especially the challenging ones. We were "typical" in that way! But I always felt safe to experience **all** of my feelings *and* to talk about them, and that message has made such a positive difference in my life. Later, as an undergraduate student majoring in child development, I was taught the same principles regarding active listening and the validation of emotions that had already been modeled for me.

Over the years, I have learned that my childhood was unusual. I know now that many people are taught that only certain feelings are acceptable and only certain feelings should be shared with others. They are told that anger itself is bad, and they are told that sadness should be hidden.

If you have learned that some emotions are okay and some are not, then I hope that you will be open to changing that perspective, because doing so will help you immensely in your recovery. I hope that you will start to believe that you have a right to feel **all** emotions. You have a right to talk about them. You have a right to find others who will listen to you and validate you. And no matter what kind of abuse you endured— whether it was emotional or physical or both, whether it occurred for a few months or many years—your feelings and your pain are just as real and all-consuming as anyone else's feelings and pain. (For more about this, please refer to the excellent article entitled "Comparing Our Losses to the Losses of Others," the link to which is listed in the Appendix.)

If you have not yet found the validation you need, please do not give up hope. There are people out there who *will* listen and give you that support. There are people out there who can provide you with specific strategies for how to cope effectively with feelings that may overwhelm you (I will discuss this more in a later chapter about trauma). In the meantime, know that you feel what you feel for a reason, and it makes you the special and normal human being that you are. In fact, when you allow yourself to feel the full range of your emotions, and when you are able to face pain, you will find that they serve as keys to unlocking the door to your inner self.

4
Introspection

Why ME?

For a long time, I felt so much shame about how easily I was duped and manipulated by the psychopath, and I wondered why I became involved in such a disturbing situation in the first place. At the same time I was asking WHY the psychopath did what he did, I was also asking myself, "Why ME? Why did he choose me? Why did I choose him? What was so wrong with me that made me a good target?" The questions were endless, and I remember being so upset with myself. Although I did not personally endure any direct projection from the psychopath, I realize that many survivors have experienced severe emotional abuse. Sometimes the abuse also includes physical violence or threats of violence. It is no wonder that survivors feel so devastated, confused, and worthless! In addition, the many ways in which psychopaths play mind games with us is the main reason why we start to believe that something must be inherently wrong with us—e.g., we are psychopath magnets—and that is why we were targeted. BUT, this is just not true.

The process of introspection is absolutely necessary for long-lasting healing, and I will share some details about my own self-awareness journey. However, I have discovered that it is very common for survivors to take on *way* too much responsibility for things that happened during their encounters with abusers, and that can be detrimental to recovery. We also unfortunately live in a world that tends to blame the victim, which may be partially due to the fact that many people do not have their eyes open to the hidden evil around them. Victim blaming—in its obvious and subtle forms—further traumatizes survivors. In order to counteract the damage, I am sharing the following four insights about psychopathic abuse and its aftermath:

Anyone can be a target

It really is true: ANYONE can be targeted by a psychopath. ANYONE can be deceived. In his book *Without Conscience*, Dr. Robert Hare writes about his first meeting with a psychopath. It happened while he was working as a psychologist in a prison, and he mentions that the prisoner knew just how to play him. In fact, writes Dr. Hare, this particular prisoner had the frightening ability to con *everyone*. It seems clear that if psychologists like Robert Hare can be so easily manipulated, then absolutely anyone can! Also, most people cannot see the truth about psychopathic evil until they have been hurt by it. And when they are hurt, they are often so confused and feel such shame that they do not share their stories with others. They keep those stories inside, and I suspect that many of them have no idea what has happened to them. Thus, the general lack of awareness about psychopathy gives predators even more opportunities to lure in victims.

Be gentle with yourself

Just by reading this book, you have taken courageous strides toward getting better! You have open eyes—you are seeing the truth about evil—and that is the first step of a survivor's quest. So try to be very kind to yourself about what happened during the en-counter **and** about the ups and downs that you will inevitably go through as you recover. Be gentle with yourself, and strive to be your own best friend. And, try to **give yourself plenty of time to heal**. It matters what you do with the time, but in many ways the process cannot be rushed. I also want to reiterate that any "obsession" you may have with the topic of psychopathy is **okay**. You can be introspective, and *focus on you*, at the very same time you learn about psychopaths. It really is possible to read about psy-chopathy AND learn about yourself at a deeper level, **all at the same time**. I know it is possible, because that is exactly how I recovered.

The abuse was not your fault!

I do not think this point can be emphasized enough: ***the abuse was not your fault***. It is so important to separate the crazy-making behaviors that the psychopath inflicted on you from the things you may have done as reactions to those behaviors. Psychopaths set us up for destruction from the very beginning by convincing us that they care so much about us, and then they revel in tearing us down by betraying us in countless ways. Normal human beings are unable to think straight in such situations! And, even if you saw red flags or had hints that something was not right, there was no way you could have known that your discomfort meant that you had encountered evil. The red flags you saw (if you saw any) could have been explained countless ways. They did not automatically translate into pathological lying, serial cheating, projection, smear campaigns, and a multitude of other cruel behaviors. You can only truly see the combination of red flags and understand their implications when you learn about how psychopaths operate, apply that information to your own experiences, and start putting the puzzle pieces together.

Each survivor is unique

Psychopaths follow a very predictable pattern in their interactions with others (idealize, devalue, discard), and in many ways certain conclusions can be made about all of them. They often are very "cookie cutter" in how they behave. Survivors, on the other hand, are much more unique, because they are normal, emotional human beings. As I mentioned above, anyone can be a target of a psychopath. That means that survivors have a range of personalities, backgrounds, interests, perceptions, strengths, weaknesses, and so on. Therefore, despite the importance of the creepy similarities across all survivor stories, the differences matter too, in terms of the process of introspection. Each person requires an individualized approach. You will probably receive a lot of advice from various people about who you are and who you should be and how you should heal, but ultimately any questions you ask yourself need to be tailored to what feels right to you. In the end, only the voice within you can tell you who you really are. Listening to *all* of your feelings and facing the pain as much as you are able are excellent strategies for tuning in to that voice. The following chapters will provide more suggestions.

Although I cannot give you any easy answers for how to look within, I can tell you that if you feel insecure, or ashamed, or stupid, or damaged, or ugly, or just utterly "less than"...you are not alone. There are countless other people who struggle with precisely those feelings and thoughts about themselves. Many of them have never been touched by evil, and if some have, they are often unable to face the truth about what has happened. I also believe that *all* normal human beings wonder if they are good enough, at one time or another. In later chapters, I will provide strategies that you can follow to feel better about yourself, but I hope that you will find comfort in knowing that you are **not** alone! My own healing journey has taught me that in many, many ways.

My Self-Awareness Quest

When he was idealizing me in the beginning, the psychopath told me more than once, "I think your self-awareness is a strength that you have." After the discard, that comment echoed in my head over and over again. Was he mocking me? Had I been delusional to think that I knew who I was when I met him? I felt so stupid and so worthless, and I was haunted by the thought that I never knew myself at all.

I eventually realized that he told me that because he was mirroring me. He listened to the many things I shared about myself, he determined which of those things I viewed as important, and then he reflected them back to me. It was indeed a cruel manipulation tool, and in many ways he **was** mocking me, but it was not a specific judgment about who I am as a person. Although his exploitation of me was tailored just for me, it was not actually personal at all. He uses the same copycat approach in all of his interactions with other people.

As I healed, I also discovered that many aspects of the fake persona he presented to me showcased the best, very *real* parts of ME, parts that he hijacked. Thankfully, I have been able to reclaim them. Those qualities existed within me before the encounter and they have been nurtured in many ways since the discard.

I also eventually realized that I **did** know myself before I met the psychopath, as much as I could at the time. To elaborate on that, I would like to share an essay I wrote during my recovery, entitled "Reflections on Self-Awareness." I wrote it while I was still feeling a lot of pain and an overwhelming compulsion to learn about psychopathy. It demonstrates that it is very possible to reflect on and learn about who we are, throughout our recoveries and throughout our lives:

If there was one thing I was sure about when I met the psychopath, it was that I knew myself. I knew my strengths and weaknesses; I understood the good points and the not-so-good points of my personality. I knew I was kind, open-minded, and sincere. I knew I was thoughtful and regularly focused on my feelings—analyzing them, processing them, and learning from them. I knew I was a good listener and a good communicator. I knew I was a perfectionist and liked to have certain things "my way." I knew I was an introvert and enjoyed my alone time. I knew I was conscientious, reliable, and responsible. I knew that I connected with others via deep, meaningful conversations. And I **also** knew I had a tendency to doubt myself and struggled with insecurities, especially about my physical appearance.

I knew all of the above about myself when the psychopath came into my life. I even knew that I should listen to my gut, having identified the misgivings I had when I became involved with a few other men before the psychopath and observed the unsuccessful outcomes of those relationships. But that gut feeling can be a hazy one if we do not trust ourselves. It can be hard to listen to our intuition when we are insecure, especially in terms of our desirability as a potential mate. I did not trust myself. I was deeply insecure, more than I realized. And what I knew in my heart but did not want to admit to myself at the time was that I wanted a relationship VERY, VERY much. I did not fully comprehend the intensity of that desire. I knew I was shy, I knew I found dating stressful, and I knew that I longed for a partner. I might have even been aware, to a small degree, that I envied my married friends. And quite frankly, my biological clock was ticking. I wanted a family! All of this, I see now, made it likely that I would—unknowingly—rush into a dangerous situation.

What I did NOT realize then was that the world is teeming with human predators. I did not know that these predators can seem "normal." I did not know that their sole purpose in life is to exploit others—emotionally and/or financially and/or physically—in a never-ending series of sick mind games based on lies. I did not know that there are human beings who are barely human, who are unable to feel the full range of emotions, who are literally incapable of loving and connecting with others in any meaningful way, and who have **no conscience**. And I really did not know that evil can be cloaked in a very intelligent, seemingly insightful and considerate package.

In retrospect, I WAS self-aware, *as much as I could be at the time*. I was naïve. I was not aware of the complex nature of humanity. I was missing important information because of my tendency to isolate myself, because I was blessed to have loving parents who never lied to me and never abused me, because I did not know that the bullying I endured as a child was a manifestation of the evil I would come across in the future, because I never healed from that trauma and was left feeling inadequate enough to be victimized again years later, in a different way, in a different form. And so I **could not see** the lies for what they were. I was distracted by the compliments and the mirroring. I became emotionally invested and made allowances for behavior I should have rejected. And I **did not know** that this person who had taken such an interest in me had completely sadistic motives and was deliberately trying to hurt me.

Psychopaths are good at blending in. Many, many people are unaware of the evil that is right in front of their faces. I was one of those people. My encounter with a psychopath has been a gift in so many ways. It has given me a depth of understanding about myself and the world that never would have been possible before. It has given me the opportunity to heal from my *whole* past and develop the love for, confidence in, and trust in myself that I need and never had.   And most importantly, it has re-taught me that life truly is a journey.   There is so much more to learn about the world and myself, each and every day.

PHASE TWO:
EVIL EVERYWHERE

"It is by suffering that human beings become angels."

~Victor Hugo

5
Trauma

PTSD

Excruciating emotional pain. Numbness. Loss of appetite. Sleepless nights. Obsessive thoughts. Inability to concentrate. Loss of pleasure in cherished activities. Lack of energy. Anxiety and panic attacks.

All of the above describe what often happens after an abusive relationship or any kind of trauma. In the chapter on pain, I mentioned how I struggled with insomnia and loss of appetite. I lost ten pounds very quickly. The weight loss should have made me happy, but I was numb and unable to find pleasure in buying smaller clothes, which had always been exciting for me in the past. I also was consumed by thoughts of the psychopath and the other woman. When I visited another state for two weeks to see my family, I had separation anxiety when it was time to leave. I hugged my mother at the airport and cried and cried; like a child, I felt actual fear about letting her go! And of course, I was overwhelmed by pain. I felt as if I could barely get through each minute, let alone an entire day.

If you can relate to much of what I have written above, you are most likely suffering from symptoms of Post Traumatic Stress Disorder (PTSD). As a disclaimer, I am not a mental health professional, and I also was not diagnosed with PTSD, although I believe I had some form of it. I will discuss the subject of therapy below, and I suggest that every survivor consider seeing a professional. I did, and it turned out that an official PTSD diagnosis was not needed in order for me to get the proper support. But such a diagnosis may be beneficial for you, and it may get you the help you need. Before I was touched by evil, it never would have occurred to me that being on the receiving end of another person's lies could produce significant trauma. But it did.

One of the most frustrating aspects of the aftermath of psychopathic abuse are the obsessive thoughts that constantly race through your mind. The thoughts are the result of the trauma (or traumas) that you have endured. You may be very tempted to do everything you can to frantically push away those thoughts and fill your days with distractions. However, as I have already mentioned, avoidance strategies do not work in the long-term. There is a very good chance that, no matter how busy you make yourself, the thoughts will continue to haunt you. On your own, it is possible to clear your mind to some degree, especially after time has passed without any contact with the psychopath. However, without support to process the trauma, you will probably come across unexpected triggers, and they may even happen on a regular basis.

I have my own personal experience with obsessive thoughts. I literally felt like I was losing my mind. I had no contact with the psychopath, and yet he continued to torment me and hurt me further, from the inside out! I immediately sought out a therapist, although I was concerned about doing so. I am well aware that many, many counselors do more harm than good. I have had direct experience with bad therapy over the years. To make matters worse, many therapists have a very poor understanding about psychopathy and personality disorders in general, as I mentioned in Chapter 2. It is not a surprise, then, that the first counselor I went to did not help me. And I might have stayed with that counselor much longer than I should have, if not for the fact that she cancelled one of our appointments early on. Given how much I was suffering, that was the motivation I needed to listen to the feeling of discomfort I had in my gut (my intuition!) and look for another therapist. It was one of the very best decisions I have ever made.

EMDR Therapy

What It Is

Looking back, I am struck by how fortunate I was to find my second therapist, given the way in which I stumbled across her. She was literally the first person I called from a list of counselors covered by my health insurance. I was intent on finding a therapist who understands personality disorders. So when she answered my phone call that day, I told her that I believed that my ex-boyfriend is a sociopath (e.g., psychopath). She paused, and I quickly said that I probably sounded crazy. She disagreed and told me that sociopaths can blend into society and sometimes be pillars of the community. And even though she was not actually accepting new patients, she decided, based on my concerns, to invite me in for an initial appointment.

During the first appointment, she simply listened to me. I was thrilled, because it can be difficult to find counselors who *really* listen. I told her about the psychopath, and although she said she did not know much about psychopathy, she agreed that something was indeed very wrong with him. She reassured me that his behavior was not going to change for the new woman, as I thought it might. Then she gave me an assignment to complete before our next meeting: she told me to write down ten memories from across my childhood and adulthood that were painful for me. And then she told me to write down ten additional memories that made me feel proud of myself. I walked out of her office that day feeling hopeful for the first time since the intense pain had begun.

When she told me that she planned to use the EMDR approach with me, I was very skeptical. I had no idea what it was, and even the name sounded strange: *Eye Movement Desensitization and Reprocessing*. What did that mean?? She encouraged me to go on the EMDR Institute's website and read about it;

and so I read about it.

When I read that the method has been researched and found to be especially effective for minimizing the negative effects of PTSD symptoms, I was excited, although unsure. It sounded very different from traditional talk therapy. And even though she told me that we would have time to talk and each session would be directed by the needs I had that day, I was still concerned. I thought about the machine my therapist has in her office, and I wondered how it worked, exactly. This could not possibly make much of a difference...right? But, then I remembered how I was unable to get the psychopath out of my head, how I cried daily on my drive to work, and how I still was unable to concentrate on anything, even those activities I used to love, and I decided I was open to doing whatever she suggested!

How It Works

Before beginning the "official" EMDR sessions, my therapist taught me two techniques that can be used at home to deal with obsessive thoughts and overwhelming feelings. First, she had me picture a peaceful place that was devoid of any negative memories or associations. I think of a "cozy chair" in which I can relax and read a book, in front of a warm fireplace. To bring up this image, I simply need to think of the words "cozy chair," and it takes my mind to that place. Second, she instructed me to create a "box" in my mind, into which I can place difficult thoughts and feelings. They are not permitted to come back out of the box once they are put in it, until or unless I release them. I decided to use the Pensieve from the Harry Potter books as my image.

As she taught me these techniques, she had me hold a flattened, oval-shaped "ball" in each hand; the two balls are connected to the machine I mentioned earlier. They vibrate back and forth in a regular rhythm while they are held. (Sometimes therapists use auditory tones instead of the balls.) She adjusted the intensity of the vibrations until I felt comfortable. After I learned these techniques, we were ready for the official EMDR.

My counselor knew that I was in so much pain because of the psychopath, so even though EMDR protocol suggests that the earliest difficult memory be targeted first, she decided to focus on my most recent trauma. She had me go back to our breakup conversation and asked me what images I had in my mind and what I was feeling. She asked me about the intensity of the feelings and in which part of my body I felt those emotions. She asked me what thoughts I had about myself, too. Then she encouraged me to just allow the images and thoughts in my brain to go where they wanted and needed to go. I did that, and after a little while, she stopped me and asked me to share what I was thinking. I shared, she took me back to the original memory, and we repeated the above process.

During this first session, the memory was not re-processed to adaptive resolution—in other words, the memory was still emotionally traumatic—because it was fresh and very painful. However, soon after that first session, I started to feel immediate benefits! For instance, my brain had been stimulated and continued to do some reprocessing; I had a dream two nights later about the psychopath that was a bit intense, but it was also productive and reassuring. And the following weekend, I noticed that I had the desire to accomplish something and complete a task, which felt wonderful after the constant numbness. After that first session, I certainly became a believer in EMDR!

A few of the subsequent therapy sessions involved targeting the breakup memory, but as I began to feel better and better, we focused on negative childhood memories. A few of these were each reprocessed in just one session. And my therapist guided me in strengthening the positive feelings and thoughts when a memory was on the verge of being reprocessed. I was amazed to find that, as they were reprocessed, I began to feel a new kind of lightness and self-love that I had never felt before. It is difficult to describe. I simply knew that deep and fast changes were occurring inside me—inside my brain—and I was deeply grateful.

Finding a Therapist

EMDR has completely transformed my life. After the discard, I could barely function. Today, I live a life free of traumatic triggers, and when I think about the psychopath, the pain is gone. Time has helped desensitize me to memories of the relationship, but EMDR therapy accelerated and cemented that process significantly.

As a result of EMDR, I also **automatically** feel confidence in myself, and love for myself, that I never thought was possible! Before this therapy, I really believed I would always battle deep insecurities; I figured it was an ingrained personality trait. Now I know that many of my struggles were the result of upsetting childhood memories that had been processed by my brain in ways that allowed them to remain traumatic, until they were reprocessed through EMDR.

In addition, I have never been able to meditate, and I have never been good at "visualization" exercises. I thought that the EMDR approach might require that I have those abilities, but it does not. I really believe it can work for **anyone** and **everyone**.

My counselor calls herself an EMDR therapist, not a therapist who uses EMDR. She offers two important tips for finding a **good** EMDR therapist: first, find out if the counselor uses a list of the ten most upsetting events from childhood to the current age; second, ask how often the therapist uses EMDR. The best answer to this question from a prospective therapist is, "I use it with most of my clients." If the answer is, "I use it as needed," then the counselor may not be as involved in or comfortable with this particular treatment.

If you would like more information about EMDR therapy, please refer to the recommended resources in the Appendix.

Other Methods for Resolving Trauma

EMDR therapy is, of course, just one way to find relief from the pain and obsessive thoughts. Another method that has worked well for some survivors is something called Emotional Freedom Technique (EFT), or tapping. I have included the link to an article about it in the Appendix, so please refer to that for more information. One advantage of tapping is that you can start doing it on your own, for free.

There are other methods of therapy that have been shown to be effective in treating trauma, such as trauma-focused cognitive behavioral therapy, or CBT. Another possibility is imagination therapy; the method is described in a wonderful article by Peace, entitled "My Anxiety Cure." You can find the link in the Appendix. Meditation techniques can also be very helpful, although they may not be enough to help you reprocess traumatic memories and prevent triggers.

Even if you choose not to or are unable to pursue therapy, I hope that you will somehow seek out support from others. (The resources listed in the Appendix can help you with that.) You should not have to go through this by yourself! Be aware, however, that as you seek out help, you will probably come across others who will *not* understand what you are going through. Sadly, recovery can be a very lonely road.

6
Loneliness

A Heavy Soul

The pain and horror that come with realizing that you have been abused by a psychopath is a shocking and disorienting way in which to lose your innocence. After all, you probably believed that there was the potential for good in all people. You probably believed that others feel the same emotions that you do and that they are telling the truth when they say, "I love you." And you may have even believed that evil is obviously sinister and would never be cloaked in a sweet-looking package.

The shock of discovering that those beliefs do not apply to everyone is yet another reason why you feel as if you are going crazy. You may find that you now see evil everywhere, and it will seem as if darkness has suddenly descended upon you, both outside and within. The result will be that you have what feels like a very heavy soul.

In addition, once your eyes are open, and as you learn about psychopathy and yourself, you experience "light bulb" moments, not only about the psychopath who abused you, but also about other people in your life. These moments tend to happen in quick succession at first and then slow down to more of a trickle as you learn about psychopathy. You may continue to have revelations over the course of several months or even longer. It takes a long time for your brain to adjust to your new vision. You also may begin to recognize psychopathic traits in family members, co-workers, friends, celebrities, and strangers. In many ways, having open eyes is a very isolating experience, which often leads to even more feelings of despair.

Your new understanding of the world enables you to see what you could not see before. The evil that you now see everywhere—or at least think that you see everywhere—**that evil has always existed**. However, it was hidden from you because of your innocence. Now that you are aware of this reality, it is natural for you to look at every new person with strong suspicion and brace yourself for an onslaught of hurtful behavior such as the kind you survived. You probably struggle with fear and panic because of the pain from the trauma you experienced and from the knowledge that you might be traumatized again. You are understandably wary of building new relationships with others, and you probably feel disconnected from humanity. You may find yourself longing to resurrect the innocence you once had; the world seemed so safe then, and now it seems so very dark.

Finding Validation

The burden of a heavy soul is too much to bear without emotional validation. As I mentioned in Chapter 4, during the course of your journey you will certainly come across others who will tell you what to do and how to feel. They will even tell you who you are and who you should be. If you try to talk about what has happened to you, you will almost certainly hear statements such as, "I don't understand why you keep talking about this," or "Just let it go" or "It's time for you to move on." When you share your story, others may not believe you, and they may tell you that evil does not exist.

Remember, people can usually only become aware of evil once they have been violated by it, and even that is no guarantee they will be able to accept the truth. Also, as you struggle to deal with the difficult emotions that threaten to overwhelm you, others make insensitive remarks and deny your perspective because, in doing so, many of them are attempting to avoid feeling any of the pain they are sensing from you. Thus, they turn on their own self-defense mechanisms, which unfortunately causes even more pain for all involved.

It is very upsetting to be invalidated by others in so many ways, and it may seem impossible to find other people who truly understand what you are going through. Thankfully, you **can** find others who share your new vision of the world, especially in the context of online communities. Websites like Lovefraud and PsychopathFree offer opportunities for discussion and connection with other survivors who can help alleviate some of the loneliness you may feel. The more that you can find others to validate your feelings and perceptions, the better you will heal. The genuine support from those who understand allows you to be who you truly are so that you can start to *validate yourself,* and it enables you to follow your own healing path.

When I found a community that was right for me, I actually did not feel lonely anymore, even though I was without a romantic partner. I started to feel **okay** about being alone and being single, for the first time in my life!

Aloneness is very different from loneliness. Spending time alone will give you the space you need to get to know yourself again, and it will protect you from further harm while you recover. You may also find, as I did, that embracing alone time and building loving relationships with fellow survivors, as well as others who understand you, helps you gradually see the light that **does** exist in this world.

In order to see *all* of the light, however, you must continue to push through the darkness.

7
Rage

The Truth About Anger

Your new wisdom about the evil around you, and specifically about the evil that exists within the person who abused you, inevitably results in feelings of rage. I wrote in Chapter 3 that anger is usually perceived as a "bad" emotion. You may have been taught not to talk about it or even acknowledge it. You may have been taught to stuff it down into the depths of you and/or force yourself to "let it go"—or at least, **say** that you have let it go—even though it is still festering inside you. But these are ineffective approaches to anger. It will find a way to torment you if you do not allow yourself to feel it, if you ignore it in one way or another, or if you pretend to let it go before you are ready. The truth is that anger is *not* "bad." When channeled appropriately, it has the potential to motivate all of us normal human beings to better ourselves, and it even has the potential to protect us from dangerous situations.

Although anger—and its even more intense cousin, rage—can be beneficial and facilitate healing, they are also extremely difficult emotions to process in safe ways. This becomes especially apparent while experiencing the horrific pain that is inevitable during the aftermath of psychopathic abuse.

When you see behind the psychopath's mask, and you realize the extent of the betrayal, the shock, shame, and sadness you feel give way and/or are accompanied by a burning rage. It is unique in the sense that it is very overwhelming and intense. It also lingers and comes in waves. This particular rage is also quite frightening because it can sometimes seem as if you are taking on the psychopath's evil.

For instance, during one of my EMDR therapy sessions, I unintentionally imagined myself taking some sort of heavy object and smashing it into the psychopath's face. This vision was so vivid in all of its gory details, and my anger was so strong, that I immediately felt scared, and the image stopped as abruptly as it started. Did this disturbing thought mean that I had become evil because of the psychopath? No, it did not. I was justifiably and deeply angry about what had happened to me, and my brain was doing its best to work through it, via that vision. Thus, the acknowledgement and acceptance of anger is the first step toward processing it effectively.

How to Process Anger

One downside of the extreme anger you will feel is that you may be tempted to seek revenge against the psychopath. As appealing as that idea may sound, any attempt to follow through on plans for revenge will most certainly not end well. The psychopath will not be hurt by anything you do, because he or she does not feel pain. However, the likelihood is high that *you* will be negatively affected. Thankfully, there are many other, much safer, strategies that can help you work through the rage. The following is not a comprehensive list, but it is a strong start. Some of the ideas below may be obvious, and some may not:

- It is often said that physical exercise and movement is beneficial in so many ways. It is also a great method for releasing rage. Kick boxing has been especially helpful for me because it includes a great deal of punching and kicking, and I allow my imagination to go where it needs to go as I do both.

- There are multiple forms of creative expression, all of which can be used to channel anger (and other emotions). Possibilities include dance, art, writing, and music. During two different waves of anger, I wrote scathing letters to the psychopath; although I did not send them, the writing helped. I also found it satisfying to sing along (or maybe I should say yell along) with certain angry-sounding songs when the rage was especially strong.

- It may seem strange or uncomfortable (it did to me at first), but accessing the right hemisphere of the brain is a very effective method for processing anger and pain. Possible techniques that can help you do this include

EMDR therapy, various forms of meditation, and tapping.

- It might take a while and may even happen in phases, but eventually you will probably want (and need) to throw away, give away, and even destroy any items connected with the psychopath. When you are ready to let them go, it is a good opportunity to express your anger in ways that will not hurt others. You can (safely) burn the items, smash them, crush them, or tear them into pieces (which I did with two pictures I stumbled across months after the discard). These physical acts of destruction provide important paths for the rage to flow out of you.

- As Kid President says, "sometimes you just gotta scream." Screaming really can help!

- Jackson, the author of the book *Psychopath Free* (and a great friend to me personally), coined the wonderful term, Constants, to describe people with whom you can talk openly.

Constants will listen without judgment, allow you to vent, and validate your feelings, including the anger. It is much easier said than done to find such people, but when you do, they will make such a difference in your life. Keep looking...you will find them!

The frustrating reality of rage, like all difficult emotions, is that it has a tendency to sneak up on you, even if you implement the above strategies. You may be convinced you have worked through all of it, that there cannot possibly be any left...and then something will happen that will trigger a fresh wave of anger. Every time that happens, the best thing to do is go back to the strategies listed above. It might help to mentally prepare yourself for the inevitable up and down process that characterizes grief, so that you will be ready when the anger rushes back over you again. And believe it or not, tuning into your anger (and all of your feelings) is one way you can start listening to your gut, which may be your best form of protection against future entanglements with psychopathic evil.

8
Intuition

There Are No Words

Intuition is such an unclear, hazy phenomenon, and it is virtually impossible to describe in words. However, I am attempting to do so because, over the course of my recovery, I have come to appreciate how tremendously valuable it is.

Your intuition communicates with you at many different volume levels. Sometimes it screams at you, like it did to me when the psychopath claimed to be spending a weekend "alone" near the end of the encounter. And sometimes it is like a whisper and is easy to miss.

In the beginning of my time with the psychopath, for instance, I thought that I was seeing many *good* signs in terms of his behavior toward me. He was giving me attention, but not too much. He contacted me on a very consistent and regular basis. And he seemed to understand me so well! The only discomfort I felt at that time was related to the mean ways in which he talked about **some** people, his reliance on texting, and the delay between his first message to me and our first in-person meeting. But those gut feelings were faint; I could not listen to my intuition then because I was unable to understand what it was telling me. I needed to develop new insights about myself and the world before I could do that.

Tuning In

Your intuition has cried out to you at various times in your life, just as mine has. Listening to it effectively requires practice through life experiences. Even though you may have been unable to hear it in the past, you can learn how to trust it from this point forward, especially now that you have open eyes.

One way in which to tune in better is to reflect on your gut feelings in retrospect. If your encounter with a psychopath was in the context of a romantic partnership, you can start by thinking back to the beginning of **all** of your previous relationships. Can you remember an early warning, no matter how slight, that something was wrong? Most likely, you will be able to think of at least one or two. When you have them in your mind, think carefully about them and how they connected to later problems in the relationships. The same process can be followed for other situations from your past, such as those related to work, friendships, and family connections. To ensure that what you are learning stays with you, it might help to write down the early feelings of discomfort for each example, as well as the later events. Also keep in mind that when you learn how to listen to it, intuition lets you know when **any** situation is not right for you, even if the circumstances are relatively safe.

When you identify gut feelings and the reasons for them in a variety of past experiences, you become better equipped to listen to them in the future. In addition, your new understanding of predatory behavior gives you the knowledge you need to notice the kinds of red flags that you may have missed before. By keeping that knowledge in mind, and then tuning in to your intuition, you will be able to pause and pay attention to any red flags you may see in a new person's behavior. Your gut will alert you to possible danger, your new awareness will help you make sense out of that intuitive information, and the combination of both will help you break free from future entanglements with psychopathic people, hopefully before you become emotionally involved.

And yet, even though your intuition is there to guide you, you may doubt it and/or be unable to hear it properly because you doubt yourself. Your intuition can only truly help you once you see—really see—all of the wonderful qualities you have inside of you.

PHASE THREE: MORE LIGHT THAN DARK

"Trust yourself, then you will know how to live."

~Johann Wolfgang von Goethe

9
Trust

Discovering the Beauty Within

In previous chapters, I outlined the importance of opening yourself up to pain, embracing and processing all of your emotions, resolving past traumas, and tuning into your intuition. These are all steps toward **building trust in yourself**. And when you trust yourself, then your heart will open up more easily to new, safer people. But first, you must begin to see how unique and beautiful you truly are!

Believe it or not, the story of *The Ugly Ducking*, by Hans Christian Andersen, may be the inspiration you need to appreciate how the aftermath of an encounter with evil can open a window to your soul and provide a way for you to see your own inner beauty. The story absolutely helped me, and the way in which it happened was unexpected.

One day, soon after I had developed a deeper level of self-love, I read a picture book version of *The Ugly Duckling* to a group of preschoolers. I had not read that particular fairy tale in a very long time, and I was surprised at how much my perception of it had changed because of my open eyes. Take a moment to read the following excerpt from the story:

> He thought of how he had been pursued and scorned, and now he heard them all say that he was the most beautiful of all beautiful birds. The lilacs bent their boughs right down into the water before him, and the bright sun was warm and cheering. He rustled his feathers and raised his slender neck aloft, saying with exultation in his heart, "I never dreamt of so much happiness when I was the Ugly Duckling!"

Although I had always liked *The Ugly Duckling* because it has a "happy ending," it was not my favorite fairy tale because it made me inexplicably sad. I never explored **why** it made me sad; I think it was too painful for me to do that then. But after going through such a dark time, I know I was sad because for so long I saw myself as the ugly duckling. I never imagined that I could transform myself into a beautiful swan. And yet, this horrible trauma gave me the opportunity to do that. Because of my quest, I see the significant beauty within me now. I see myself as the swan, and I feel a wonderful sense of belonging. I am able to rejoice in my own uniqueness!

That beauty is inside *every* survivor, a beauty we have possessed all along and never knew we had. So as you make your way through your own recovery journey, you have the power to discover the beauty within by seeing and accepting the following truths, a few of which may now be familiar to you:

You were not stupid, you were innocent

When you first realized the extent of the psychopath's betrayal, you probably were overwhelmed by shame. How is it that you did not see the extent of the lies and the manipulation? It is normal to feel so very stupid when reality sinks in. And it is easy to become angry with yourself for not realizing that the "love" the psychopath offered you was an illusion. This is exactly how the psychopath—master of deception—wants you to feel, yet it is not the truth! You are a loving, empathetic person. You were never taught that emotionally defective human predators are out there; you only heard about them in fairy tales or in stories of serial killers. You did not know that they walk among us, many of them seemingly normal, law-abiding citizens. You cannot protect yourself from something that you never knew existed. The ugly duckling simply did not know that he was always a swan and never a duck. He should not be blamed for his innocence, and neither should you.

It is OKAY to have insecurities and vulnerabilities

You have probably been warned that it is "bad" to be insecure or vulnerable. You may even be taught this by those who are attempting to help you heal from psychopathic abuse. Yet, struggling with insecurities and being vulnerable with others are part of what makes you a normal human being. Even the most confident people doubt themselves at times; even the most emotionally healthy people need to open up their hearts to others, *and become vulnerable*, if they want to build intimate, meaningful relationships. It is absolutely possible for you to gain new confidence and still retain the ability to let others—the **right** others—into your inner circle. The ugly duckling decided to trust a man who found him half-frozen in the snow, and he was nurtured back to health. He allowed himself to be vulnerable, even after all of the taunting and abuse he endured before that. You can do the same thing, and you should do it carefully and based on what you have learned from your experiences.

Your weaknesses *and* strengths were exploited

You may feel that the ways in which you were used by the psychopath only showcased your shortcomings. You may believe that you have unique problems that make you a psychopath magnet. You were too trusting, you lacked boundaries, you did not love yourself enough, and so on. It is certainly true that your weaknesses were exploited. But your strengths were *also* exploited. The ability to love is a strength. The ability to trust is a strength. The ability to cooperate is a strength. The ability to be kind and honest and empathetic are strengths.

A psychopath has no conscience and because of that, he or she is capable of horrific cruelty. He or she uses pity plays to capitalize on your natural desire to offer kindness and understanding. The psychopath mirrors your values and all aspects of your personality—including your positive qualities—in order to make you believe that he or she is just like you, when in fact he or she is the opposite. The psychopath sets you up in such a way so that you project your own goodness on to him or her. The ugly duckling hoped that the woman, cat, and hen he turned to for help would be as kind as he was, and he unfortunately was wrong. But that did not take away from his wonderful qualities. And in your case, being targeted by a psychopath does not mean there is anything wrong with you.

Facing the pain sets you free

In the aftermath, after you free yourself from the psychopathic bond, you are left traumatized. You are like the ugly duckling, frozen in the winter landscape. You are numb, confused, left in a fog, and you are battling very intense pain. You desperately want the pain to end, and you often do whatever you can to run away from it.

You may remember from previous chapters that avoidance and denial are normal, natural human responses to pain. All normal human beings do both, to varying degrees and for varying lengths of time. However, when you find the courage inside you to really face the pain and work through it, that is when you find freedom from the pain. It is when you experience new and life-changing joy. You cannot circle around the pain and discover the happiness you deserve. You must travel through the pain and embrace all of the challenging feelings and difficult ups and downs that are the essence of the grieving process. For a long time, it may seem as if you will always be hurting...until one day you will turn a corner and find a lovely new world you never could have imagined.

When you embrace the above truths, you discover who you are at a deeper level. And you realize that you have the ability to transform yourself in ways that psychopaths never can. You realize the beauty within you has *always* been there. You can grow and change and evolve into the special and wonderful human being you always were and always were meant to be. You have the opportunity to develop new wisdom, to embrace a new perspective, and use both to find the inner light that was hidden within you and allow that light to shine. And when you do, you will learn how to trust yourself, and you will find other people who appreciate and love you.

> *"He felt quite glad of all the misery and tribulation he had gone through, for he was the better able to appreciate his good fortune now and all the beauty which greeted him. The big swans swam round and round him and stroked him with their bills."*

The ugly duckling found his way home, and you will too.

Building New Confidence

When you start to see the beauty within, it means that you are building new confidence in yourself. It is all part of the process of finding out who you are, and when you discover YOU, *that* is "home." But, confidence-building will seem like a daunting task if the pain is still very fresh for you. Remember, try to be gentle with yourself.

When you met the psychopath, you might have felt very good about yourself and your life. And even if you were not happy then, your emotional state at that time cannot be compared to the despair you may feel now. But, there is hope! For me, the confidence I now have would not have been possible without the resolution of past traumas and the support of others who understand. It has been like a positive snowball effect: in the process of dealing with those upsetting experiences through therapy and making connections with other survivors, I focused on my pain and my feelings, I learned more about myself, I started to listen to and understand my intuition, and then I began to trust myself. The end result has been a belief in ME that I never thought was possible!

You can find amazing new confidence, too. The

best way to do so is to seek out support from others who can help you heal old wounds, who will validate you, and who will encourage you to find your own unique path toward self-awareness. It is very frightening to reach out to others and to take risks after such devastating abuse and betrayal. Be especially cautious and careful as you begin to look for that initial support. Thankfully, once you find the right help, the more you will be able to heal. The more you heal, the more you will believe in yourself. And the more you can believe in yourself, the more you will be able to open up your heart to, and put your trust in, new people.

Building self-confidence should not lead to a complete elimination of self-doubts. I absolutely still doubt myself on a regular basis, about many things. The difference between my almost crippling insecurities from before and the doubts I have now is that they no longer have the power to overwhelm me. I am able to put them in perspective. I view my doubts and remaining insecurities as a normal part of being human, and I am at peace with them now.

I have also found that the trust and confidence I have in myself, and the love I have for myself, help me establish appropriate limits, or boundaries, with others. I am no longer so concerned about others liking me, and that means that I not only know how I should be treated, I will also not accept anything less than that treatment. And if I do not receive appropriate treatment, I share my thoughts and feelings much more readily with those who are upsetting me. If they are not able or willing to meet my expectations, I am then ready to walk away.

As a result of the new limits I am setting, two of my friendships have ended. They were not toxic friendships, but they were friendships that were not working for me anymore. It hurt to let them go, and I have some residual feelings of guilt, but it has given me the time and energy to nurture connections with those friends who offer me the understanding that I need and deserve. As a result, I am now much happier in my relationships, and I am much happier with myself.

The establishment of boundaries and the ability to carefully put your trust in new people should be outcomes of the work you are doing to heal. If you are struggling with one or both, then I hope that you will go back to some of the tips I have already shared: open yourself up to your feelings and your pain, reach out to others who understand, resolve past traumas, strive to see the beauty within you, and trust and love yourself first.

Unfortunately, these steps are not a guarantee that you will never be hurt again. Future pain is inevitable. But, future involvements with psychopathic people are *not*. You might encounter predators, you might even be deceived by them, but you have the potential to spot them quickly and run away. Also, when you realize how special you truly are, your life will become more joyful, and you really will establish the relationships you have been hoping to find all along. And, amazingly, when you have faith in yourself, then you will start to believe in all of humanity again. So happiness **can** be found on the other side of the darkness. Just remember, it comes from *within*.

10
Acceptance

Closure

Based on the countless posts I have read on the
PsychopathFree forum, many survivors write that
what they want more than anything is to find closure.
Some hope that they can somehow obtain that closure
from the psychopaths who abused them. Others are
convinced that closure is absolutely impossible. **All** of
them wonder if they will ever find a way out of the
darkness.

The good news is, **YES**, closure is possible. And
no, it will definitely **not** come from the psychopaths!
Just as new confidence comes from *within*, so does
closure.

In the first several chapters of this book, I provided guidelines for the initial steps you should take to achieve closure. I suggest that you:

- **Do your best to let go of the illusion**
- **Implement the No Contact rule**
- **Safely search for answers about the psychopath who hurt you, if you feel compelled to do so**
- **Research the general topic of psychopathy**
- **Allow yourself to *feel* and *think***
- **Seek out support**

I would also like to share two more important points on a possible path toward closure. Once again, I want to remind you that this roadmap does not have a timeline, and the points can overlap:

Accept what you can and cannot control

When I learned the truth about the psychopath, I was extremely disturbed to realize that such evil exists in the world. The encounter was over, and I was deeply upset to see the psychopath move on to his new target, seemingly happy, not caring about the devastation he left behind him (me...broken me). My first reaction to this was complete heartbreak, shame, and outrage. I wanted to expose the psychopath for the monster he is. I wanted to convince the other woman to leave him. I wanted him to apologize to me and actually mean it. I wanted justice, and I wanted revenge!

However, I knew that I could not stop him from lying and manipulating and hurting others. I knew I could not convince his new target of the truth. And I knew I could not make him feel remorse for what he did to me. What I **could** do was focus on my own healing and my own life. When I made the choice to do that, one day at a time, I gradually felt happier and more peaceful. I still wage a daily struggle to relinquish the desire to control what I cannot control, but, thankfully, it is not nearly as difficult as it used to be.

You will never receive traditional "closure" from the psychopath. But the light you can discover within your own soul is **so** much better!

Trust in your own unique truth

Perhaps the most significant epiphany during my recovery came when I finally was able to believe in myself and trust in my own truth. Psychopaths are eerily similar in so many ways, and yet many of the details of my experience seemed so different from other survivors' stories.

I have already mentioned that, as I fought to make sense out of what had happened to me, I heard so many opinions from so many people about how to heal, about who I was, about who I should be, and about what to believe. I questioned myself, as I always had, and as long as my intense self-doubt remained, my pain lingered. Ironically, it was only after reading survivor story after survivor story, so similar to mine and yet so different, that the fog began to lift. Only after reading so many other stories, and only after seeing my own worth, was I able to see the truth in what happened to me. As I revealed in the previous chapter, I absolutely still have doubts, about so many things. But now I put those doubts in perspective and listen first to the voice within my heart.

You have a similar voice in your own heart. Listen to it.

And, please hold on to the following truth: you **can** find closure, and you **can** find peace on the other side of the nightmare. Follow the suggestions that I have shared, and most of all, strive daily to believe in and love yourself, **your most authentic self**. *You* are your own best guide.

Forgiveness or Acceptance?

I have struggled immensely with the issue of forgiving the psychopath. I finally realized that I have had such a hard time with it because of the many perspectives that exist regarding what, exactly, the word "forgiveness" means. I have always believed that forgiveness involves pardoning. In other words, when one says, "I forgive you," it means, "Everything is okay." And I knew that what the psychopath did to me would *never, ever* be okay.

Over the course of my recovery, I learned that other definitions of forgiveness exist. They include the following:

> "To give up resentment of or claim to requital for" and "to cease to feel resentment against"

(www.merriam-webster.com)

"Stop feeling angry or resentful toward (someone) for an offense, flaw, or mistake" (www.oxforddictionaires.com)

"To give up resentment against or the desire to punish" (www.yourdictionary.com)

Although I agree with the above definitions (and I will elaborate on why in just a moment), the fact remains that other people will make varied assumptions about what it means for me to "forgive" the psychopath. Therefore, I have chosen to abandon the word "forgiveness" entirely and use "acceptance" instead. I believe the term acceptance focuses much more on the survivor than it does on the abuser—in positive ways—and puts the control in the survivor's hands. Of course, please trust in *your* truth. If forgiveness is the term that feels right for you, then by all means embrace it and use it.

Reaching acceptance not only involves truly seeing the evil that exists in the person who abused you and in the world in general, but it also means reaching a point of letting go of any anger and resentment you may feel about that reality. I understand how difficult and even impossible that sounds. It was extremely hard for me to accomplish, and until it actually happened, I wondered if I would ever be able to let the anger go. Allow me to explain how I did it.

I want to make it very clear that I will always be appalled and disturbed that psychopathic evil exists, and I will always be disgusted by the ways in which I personally was mistreated by the psychopath who abused me. Also, before I could reach acceptance, I **FIRST** needed to fully experience the rage that I described in Chapter 7. I needed to **hate** him. I needed to write nasty letters that I never sent, I needed to talk about what happened and "obsess" about it, and I needed to cry until it felt as if I had no tears left.

Then, after more than a year of being angry, and after implementing all of the strategies I shared about working through rage, I began to realize that the psychopath—and all others like him—still had a certain level of power and control over me, as long as I held on to the resentment. And, in my case, I noticed it was **so easy** to hold on to it. But I realized that I had the power of choice: I could *choose* to let it go. For me, it helped to follow a symbolic ritual, during which I threw a small rock representing my residual anger into a nearby pond. I was given the rock many months after the discard, and I actually held on to that rock for several *more* months before I felt ready to let it go.

If you are angry right now, and you cannot imagine letting go of that anger, it is okay! You may not be ready yet. There is no particular timeline for how long the anger should last. Just know that it *is* possible to reach a point at which the anger is less intense. You might even find, like I did, that when you reach that point, the anger itself feels like a burden. Although I had already made wonderful progress in my recovery by then, I noticed that the anger was weighing me down. If you start to have similar feelings, that is when you will know that you can choose to let the rage go. And when you do, you will find freedom. You will feel indifference toward the psychopath, you will feel lighter and happier, and you will also more easily see the good in others again.

11
Love

Seeing the Good Again

One day, as I struggled with my heavy soul and the burden of seeing the evil around me, and as I battled feelings of despair, I had a quiet revelation. I realized that, just as I could choose to let go of the anger, I could also choose to believe, based on my research of psychopathy and my own life experiences, that there are many more normal and good people than there are evil people in the world. And I could choose to believe that love **will** triumph, because all normal human beings have a deep need to establish meaningful relationships with others.

Soon after I made the choice to believe that I will

find more light than dark, a wonderful thing happened. I started seeing—really seeing—more kindness and compassion in the actions of the people around me. I also found that, as I was able to gradually see the good again, I felt more joy and more gratitude as a result.

An intimate encounter with evil changes you forever. It is completely okay to mourn your lost innocence, yet you cannot retrieve it. You will find that your soul will feel darkened by the experience, but it does not need to be a permanent change! The truth is that more good than evil exists in this world. There are many, many people out there who feel *all* emotions, who are capable of compassion, and who are able to experience real love. Once you have worked through the pain of what has happened to you, had your feelings validated, built yourself back up, and discovered that you are not alone in your new understanding of humanity, you can start to see the good again. Just like the dark, the light has always been there, and it will be waiting for you to embrace it...when you are ready.

The Power of Love

It may seem as if psychopaths really do have an unfair advantage. They manipulate and exploit other people in order to get what they want, and in many ways, they *do* get what they want, especially in the short-term. They clearly seem to achieve what they covet most of all: victory and "winning." That is why survivors might wonder, does love really make a difference?

I realize that not everyone is a fan of the Harry Potter books, but I believe that the following quote, from *Harry Potter and the Order of the Phoenix*, by J.K. Rowling, epitomizes how good **does** always win. It is a statement Professor Dumbledore made to Harry, and it demonstrates the incredible power of love:

> *"There is a room in the Department of Mysteries that is kept locked at all times. It contains a force that is at once more wonderful and more terrible than death, than human intelligence, than forces of nature. It is also, perhaps, the most mysterious of the many subjects for study that*

reside there. It is the power held within that room that you possess in such quantities and which Voldemort has not at all. That power took you to save Sirius tonight. That power also saved you from possession by Voldemort, because he could not bear to reside in a body so full of the force he detests. In the end, it mattered not that you could not close your mind. It was your heart that saved you."

Yes, Harry Potter is fiction. But J.K. Rowling's stories encompass so many truths about the world in which we live. They demonstrate that love *does* make a difference, and they demonstrate that love has the power to defeat psychopathic evil, in the end. Those who are capable of love are able to transform themselves and evolve into better human beings. They can build true communities and make **real** connections with each other. In contrast, and just like Voldemort (the antagonist in the stories), psychopaths are limited, empty, and soulless. Like Voldemort, they are cursed with a half-life.

Although I have been scarred by the cruelty that I have experienced at different points over the years, I have also been wonderfully protected by the love given to me by others. I have had the gift of my parents' love throughout my life, I have had teachers who inspired me through their small gestures of kindness and praise for my abilities, and I have found friends who accept me for who I am, who celebrate with me when I am successful, and who support me when I am down. And so the psychopath did not destroy me. The aftermath of the encounter gave me the opportunity to make myself even better, because I can love and he cannot. Harry Potter's world was saved by the cumulative effect of the love that caring people offered one another. And our world can be saved in the same way.

It can be extremely overwhelming to think about the horrific ways in which psychopaths orchestrate their evil agendas. But those of us who have open eyes cannot close them; we cannot undo what we now see. We can find the courage within us and strive to accept the truth, as beautiful and terrible as it often is. We can be like phoenixes, reborn from the ashes of our lost innocence. And in doing so, we find hope and healing. We find others who understand. We find friends who sincerely love us, and we find out who we really are, allowing our inner light to shine. We come together to fight for what is right and true, we find compassion for those who deserve it, and we help each other along this often difficult and lonely path. And when we are able to believe in the amazing power that we have within us, we realize that the world is full of love and light and the promise that good will always triumph over evil.

Epilogue

More than a year after the discard, as I was or-
ganizing some of my old keepsakes, I came across a
short story I had written while I was in my late teens,
a piece of fantasy fiction. For some reason, I decided
to take a moment to read through it, which I had literally not done since I had written it. By the time I
reached the end, I noticed that I was crying. The content of the story showed me that somehow, all those
years ago, I already knew exactly what I needed to
achieve during my survivor's quest: a deep conviction
that I *am* good enough.

I have decided to include that short story as a
symbol of my personal journey. (Please be aware that,
because I wrote it while I was a teenager, it has a

116

teenager's perspective, despite some slight changes.) Perhaps you will see yourself in the story, and if you do, may it inspire you to believe in your own unique worth.

The Forest

The swaying branches of the tall trees loomed high overhead as I carefully picked my way across the forest floor, sidestepping fallen twigs and avoiding poison ivy and sumac as best I could. Stopping for a moment, I gazed upward and discovered that the bright June sun barely penetrated through the dense leaves. I continued on after a while, smiling softly to myself. The outside problems of the human race miraculously disappeared as one stepped into the wilderness of a forest.

This particular forest I thought of as my own. Ever since I was a small child, I had always used it as a refuge from my problems at home that had been, and still were, plentiful. To reach it, I need only walk through my backyard. I can still hear my mother's voice calling after me those many times I decided to flee. "Cassandra, don't go too far! Who knows what kind of awful things are in the woods. Please, Casey, be careful!" I would calmly wave my hand and hurry off. My parents owned many acres of land, including a large portion of the forest (if you can *really* own a forest), so I never felt I was trespassing. The calming atmosphere, with sounds of scurrying animals and rustling plants, always put me at ease after a long day. I especially craved the sanctuary when my older brother, Kyle, trifled with my feelings, as he often did. His teasing usually reinforced my own private opinion of myself. That day, however, I simply enjoyed the nature that surrounded me and attempted to put my difficult emotions aside.

After walking for a distance, I came upon a large, familiar rock, one lined with dewy moss. The vegetation was comfortable, and I settled myself on top of the cushion. I leaned my head against a nearby tree and closed my eyes, listening to the various sounds that surrounded me. I felt so peaceful and content that soon nature's music acted as a lullaby and gently eased me into a light slumber.

Sleeping peacefully, I was at first unaware of the small hand that jiggled my arm persistently. Soon, however, I awakened to find an extremely beautiful girl beside me. Confused, I stared at her in disbelief. I asked, rising slowly, "Who are you?"

The girl smiled and replied kindly in a silvery voice, "I'm Malinda. Who are you?"

Thrown off guard by the unexpected answer, I awkwardly recited my name. I stopped and stared at the girl. Malinda looked to be about eight years old, and yet, when she had spoken, her voice sounded mature and all-knowing. As I stared and attempted to determine exactly what was happening, Malinda took my hand and pulled me to my feet. Surprised, I asked breathlessly, "Where are we going?" Malinda smiled but did not reply. As the girl walked, small particles of surreal dust floated into the air behind her. I watched, fascinated, and stumbled as I was pulled along. I felt as if I were inside a mysterious dream world.

Before long we reached a clearing, on which stood a number of houses. People were roaming various walkways and tending small, pretty gardens. Each person was an incredibly gorgeous child, with creamy skin, sparkling eyes, and thick, healthy hair that shined. As I observed this and searched for a logical explanation, Malinda again pulled on my arm. Reluctantly, I followed, and, after many twists and turns, was led to a small cabin. Two tall maple trees rested comfortably on either side, and smoke calmly billowed from the chimney of the cozy establishment. Many forest animals were busily playing with each other as I looked on. The creatures were not at all troubled by the presence of me or my guide. I allowed myself to relax slightly, although I was still greatly puzzled. I asked Malinda, "Could you please tell me what exactly I'm doing here?"

Malinda smiled and said simply, "You have been chosen, Casey Hawkins."

I stared at the mysterious girl. "For what?" She said nothing.

I felt myself becoming slightly alarmed, and my heartbeat suddenly quickened. I frowned. What kind of strange place had I come to? What did these people want from me? Why had I been chosen, and for what? As I pondered the questions tumbling around inside my head, a soft, clear, soprano voice floated through the air and startled me out of my reverie. I looked up and realized I was now inside the cottage at which Malinda and I had been gazing. I quickly looked around, wondering how I had been transported from the strange world outside to the equally baffling inside of the cabin. Another young girl was seated in a rocking chair with her back turned toward the two of us.

She was singing a slow, comforting melody as she swayed back and forth, unaware that anyone was in her home. Her voice was flawless.

"Who is that?" I whispered to Malinda, my worries forgotten for the moment.

Malinda's face softened tenderly. "She is the Ancient One."

"What? But she's just a child!" I was incredulous. Malinda was silent, her genuine smile never faltering.

As we watched, the Ancient One slowly turned. She was far more beautiful than I had ever imagined another person to be, and she was younger than all of the others that dwelled inside the peculiar village. I stared at the person before me, astounded, attempting to control my frayed nerves. Soon, however, the rapidly changing, unbelievable things I had seen and experienced were too much for me to bear. To me, it made absolutely no sense. I decided it was time I left this perplexing world.

"Excuse me," I said angrily, "but I'm a little confused. I was just taking a nice nap when suddenly, here I am, stuck in this weird little village. I swear, it's like a page out of Alice in Wonderland!" I crossed my arms. "I want to go home."

The Ancient One, paying no attention to my outburst, smiled. "But you, my dear, are the chosen one."

I scowled. "What does that *mean*?"

"Why, the wisdom tree has spoken. Its words are in the grass and the trees and the air. They are in the entire forest that surrounds us. It has said that you are to be the one. So, you see, you cannot leave." The Ancient One, seeing my blank look, said quietly, with an even brighter smile lighting up her beautiful face, "Come, I will show you."

Leaving Malinda behind, the girl and I walked through the small back door of the cabin and out into the sunshine. We traveled down a narrow, densely wooded path until we reached another clearing, in the center of which stood a small willow tree, its stems and leaves swaying gently in the breeze.

"This," I said slightly sarcastically as I stared at the vegetation, "is the wisdom tree?"

"Yes, my child. We knew some day you would come and fulfill its purpose."

I sighed. "Why did it pick me?"

The Ancient One smiled. "That is for you to discover. The tree will help you."

I glanced skeptically at the plant. The Ancient
One, catching my uncertain look, touched my arm.
"Do not worry, my dear. The answers are inside of
you." She vanished.

I stood at the edge of the clearing and stared at
the tiny tree. I wondered, for the tenth time, what in
the world I was doing there, and who, or what, had
brought me. I could think of no way to find out.

Hesitantly, I walked toward the tree, studying its
every feature. I stopped when I was near its branches
and reached out to take a leaf in my hand. I held it for
a moment and then dropped it to the ground. It flut-
tered downward slowly before it was finally still.
Nothing happened, as I had expected; there were no
surprises, no sudden explosions or surreal voices,
from the fallen leaf, or from the rest of the tree. I sat
down on the bed of grass at my feet and touched a
piece of bark on the trunk of the tree. I paused.
Again, all was still. I sighed.

"So, why did you want me so much?" I said to the

tree. I suddenly became philosophical. "I mean, I'm honored, but what made me so special that you chose me? *Me*, over everyone else in the world. There were so many to pick from, you know? How did you decide? Was it that award I got for gymnastics that pushed me over the top? Or was it the A I got on my English final?" I stared intensely at the tree, probing its depths. "Or was it simply the fact that I love this forest so much that it hurts?" I was silent for a moment. Then I laughed at myself. "This is ridiculous. I just said the cheesiest thing ever, and I said it to tree! I think I may be losing it." I felt like a fool. I shrugged my shoulders and slowly got to my feet, turning away from the strange plant. I began walking.

Suddenly, a flash of light caught my eye. I faced the tree for a second time and watched, transfixed, as it merged into an odd shape. I soon realized I was staring at myself in some kind of remarkable mirror. Awed at what had happened, I studied my too-thin fifteen-year-old body, enclosed in shorts and a t-shirt and gazed at my familiar big brown eyes and long, thick auburn hair. The edges of the mirror changed shape rapidly, as if, at any moment, the entire object would collapse. I was transfixed by the sight, and yet, amid the unbelievable happenings of the tree, I concluded something astonishing: I was different! But how?

To my surprise, I found that I actually *knew* the answer! Throughout my entire life, I had been out of sync with my peers; I had always wished to be part of the popular crowd, the one that was "in the know," the same one I had been excluded from time and time again. I had never been cool enough, smart enough, pretty enough. I had just never been *good* enough. And suddenly, as I observed my reflection in the wide mirror of the wisdom tree, the desperate goal of being accepted seemed not so important anymore. It seemed not to matter, for I had discovered something very powerful within myself, something so simple, I wondered why I hadn't noticed it before. For the first time in my life, I had view my reflection, my face, body, and hair, without cringing. I had, for an instant, *liked* what I'd seen!

Excited, I turned toward the tree, eager to glimpse once again the changed image of myself. I found, however, the tree to be gone, and in its place the ordinary green needles of a pine. I whirled around and found the moss-covered rock settled in a patch of grass, undisturbed. I was not troubled, though. I sprang up and hurried toward home.

I opened the front door of my house and yelled inside. Waiting for a moment, I concluded that nobody was at home. Slightly disappointed, for I was eager to share my news with *someone*, I started up the flight of steps to the second floor. I had reached the middle of the staircase when a voice called out at me.

"Hey, loser. Watcha been doin'?" I turned to find my brother Kyle grinning up at me. Before I could answer, he said sarcastically, "Oh, I forgot. You couldn't have been doin' much because you don't have a life!" He then cracked up at his own lame remark.

Anger swelled up inside of me, and the old insecurities of the past years flooded my mind. I opened my mouth, but I found I had nothing to say. I snapped it shut, and my face muscles relaxed. I knew, in my head, that Kyle was simply attempting to make me react in a negative way to his put-downs, which I usually did. I knew it was great entertainment for him. And, even though I was hurt by his teasing, I instead decided not to play into his hands. I said shortly, "I've been in the forest, actually."

Kyle snorted. "You've been talkin' to the animals, huh? Well, I can understand that." He gazed at me in mock sympathy. "After all, they *are* your only friends." He began snickering at me once more.

I stared at my older brother and was disgusted by what I saw. Merely two years my senior, he often acted as if he was much younger than his age. He had constantly snubbed and made fun of me in the past, just as he was doing now. But, for once, I was not upset. I was only annoyed. My lips turned upward into a smile. I said, with a great deal of mock affection, "You know, Kyle, even with all your faults, I still love you." Before he could come up with another snide remark, I turned and climbed my way to the top of the stairs. I could feel Kyle's eyes staring after me.

Early the next morning, as soon as the sun had shone its bright light over the horizon, I was picking my way through the woods. My mother, of course, had called out to me as I rumbled down the stairs and pulled on my hiking boots. "Where are you going now?" she had asked.

"To the forest, Mom." I heard her sigh and mutter softly, "She'll get all dirty..." as I slipped on my coat and slammed the door. I then skipped off the porch, in the direction of the trees. Deeply curious about what had happened the day before, I now traveled until I arrived at the spacious rock. Placing myself comfortably upon it, I listened as the birds conversed with each other and wondered if my experience had all been a dream. Had my meeting with the magical children possessing untimely beauty been real? I shook my head; it just wasn't possible.

A patch of leaves rustled behind me. I turned, expecting to see a squirrel scampering into the brush. Instead, I watched as a cloud of dust slowly settled on to a soft patch of grass. I stared at the spot for a long time; then, I slowly turned and rose from the rock. I gazed through the pine needles in the direction of the mythical place that I, Casey, had been chosen to witness. As I stared off into the distance, I realized this wilderness I so loved was truly a magical place. It was not the faraway, perhaps even non-existent village and people I had encountered that made it so incredible; it was simply the life within its walls of trees and plants that gave it its extraordinary atmosphere. I felt honored that its powers had chosen to show me a way to love myself as much as I loved it. I closed my eyes and took a deep breath, smiling to myself. Then, after one more glance at the piece of ground nestled by the rock, I pushed a branch aside and continued on through the forest.

Acknowledgements

I want to express my deepest gratitude and love to the following people:

The members of the PsychopathFree online community, especially my fellow administrators and moderators, as well as the few members with whom I connected from the very beginning. This book would not exist without their stories, their wisdom, their understanding, and their love.

My parents. Their endless support and profound love over the years have made it possible for me to achieve countless goals and dreams.

My close friends, some of whom I have known for years, and some of whom came into my life after the encounter. All of them have restored my belief in humanity.

My therapist. Like Casey's forest, she taught me how to finally believe that I AM good enough. And she taught me how to give as much love and kindness to *myself* as I try to give to others.

Appendix

Recommended Resources

The following is a list of resources that I highly recommend. The content of Chapter 2, in particular, is based on the information I learned from the books and websites that are listed. Please note that the books and articles are listed in alphabetical order. You can of course find many more resources via a Google search, and I encourage you to conduct as much research as you feel you need. Many of the resources I have included below were especially meaningful to me, and they represent an excellent starting point for learning and support.

General Books About Psychopathy and Recovery:

Dangerous Liaisons: How to Recognize and Escape from Psychopathic Seduction, by Claudia Moscovici

Psychopath Free: Recovering from Emotionally Abusive Relationships With Narcissists, Sociopaths, & Other Toxic People, by Peace

(A second edition of *Psychopath Free* is due to

**be published and made available in bookstores
in 2015, under a different title and under the author name of Jackson MacKenzie. At that time,
the original version listed here will no longer be
available.)**

*Red Flags of Love Fraud—10 Signs You're Dating a
Sociopath*, by Donna Andersen

The Sociopath Next Door, by Martha Stout, Ph.D.

*Without Conscience: The Disturbing World of the
Psychopaths Among Us*, by Robert D. Hare, Ph.D.

Specialized Books About Psychopathy:

Discarded: One Mother's Journey with a Psychopath,
by Indie Mom

Snakes in Suits: When Psychopaths Go to Work, by
Paul Babiak, Ph.D. and Robert D. Hare, Ph.D.

Resources About Introspection:

*The Gifts of Imperfection: Let Go of Who You Think
You're Supposed to Be and Embrace Who You Are*, by
Brené Brown, Ph.D.

Brené Brown, *The Power of Vulnerability*, TED Talk:
https://www.youtube.com/watch?v=iCvmsMzlF7o

Additional Information About EMDR Therapy:

Getting Past Your Past: Take Control of Your Life with Self-Help Techniques from EMDR Therapy, by Francine Shapiro, Ph.D.

EMDR International Association **(visit this website first if you are interested in finding a therapist)**: www.emdria.org

EMDR: Mind-body therapy aids trauma victims: http://www.gazettenet.com/living/health/10514350-95/emdr-mind-body-therapy-aids-trauma-victims

EMDR Institute, Inc.: www.emdr.com

5 EYEWITNESS News Report on EMDR Therapy: https://www.youtube.com/watch?v=QWnj9QQbD8c

The Evidence on EMDR: http://consults.blogs.nytimes.com/2012/03/02/the-evidence-on-e-m-d-r/

Can You Benefit from EMDR Therapy? http://psychcentral.com/lib/2012/can-you-benefit-from-emdr-therapy/

General Websites about Psychopathy:

www.psychopathfree.com *(includes a very active forum and a library of articles)*

psychopathyawareness.wordpress.com *(includes a*

variety of articles)

www.lovefraud.com *(includes a blog that is open to comments, as well as many articles)*

18orule.com *(includes articles that are open to comments)*

www.aftermath-surviving-psychopathy.org *(includes general information about psychopathy and a link to a radio show about psychopathy; all information comes from experts in the field)*

A Sample of Helpful Articles:

Comparing Our Losses to the Losses of Others:
http://www.lovefraud.com/2012/05/04/comparing-our-losses-to-the-losses-others/

Cutting Ourselves Some Slack:
http://www.lovefraud.com/2010/10/21/cutting-ourselves-some-slack/

Dangerous Mind Games: How Psychopaths Manipulate and Deceive:
https://psychopathyawareness.wordpress.com/category/dangerous-mind-games-how-psychopaths-manipulate-and-deceive/

EFT Tapping Helps You Deal with the Trauma of Sociopaths:
http://www.lovefraud.com/2013/02/04/eft-tapping-helps-you-deal-with-the-trauma-of-sociopaths/

Finally Free: The Courage to Be Me:
https://www.psychopathfree.com/content.php?285-
Finally-Free-The-Courage-to-Be-Me

The Gray Rock Method of Dealing with Psychopaths:
http://180rule.com/the-gray-rock-method-of-
dealing-with-psychopaths/

*How Can I Forgive You? The Courage to Forgive, the
Freedom Not to:*
http://psychopathyawareness.wordpress.com/2011/1
0/29/how-can-i-forgive-you-the-courage-to-forgive-
the-freedom-not-to/

My Anxiety Cure (or Maybe PTSD Cure?):
https://www.psychopathfree.com/content.php?254-
My-Anxiety-Cure-(Or-Maybe-PTSD-Cure-)

*Overcoming Brainwashing and the Sociopath's
World of Lies:*
https://www.psychopathfree.com/content.php?283-
Overcoming-Brainwashing-and-the-Sociopath-s-
World-of-Lies

*Why Does It Take So Long to Get Over a Relationship
with a Psychopath?:*
https://www.psychopathfree.com/content.php?270-
Why-Does-it-Take-So-Long-to-Get-Over-a-
Relationship-with-a-Psychopath

*Why We Need to Talk About Our Experiences with
Sociopaths:*
http://www.lovefraud.com/2014/06/23/why-we-
need-to-talk-about-our-experiences-with-sociopaths/

ABOUT THE AUTHOR

HealingJourney is a teacher of young children, an enthusiastic reader, and an occasional writer. She appreciates thoughtful conversations, alone time, swimming, and chocolate. She is also one of the administrators of the PsychopathFree forum. You can email her at healingjourney@psychopathfree.com.

Made in the USA
Columbia, SC
31 May 2020